The Secret to

Retirement Planning is

THERE IS NO '$ECRET'!

A Guide
for Financial
Professionals

LARRY GEORGE

To the millions of Baby Boomers on the verge of retirement, who are anxiously fretting about the what's, when's and how's of formulating a happy, successful plan for enjoying their non-working years.

TABLE OF CONTENTS

Foreword   page i

Introduction   page iii

Chapter One .... page 1
   WHY SHOULD YOU DO RETIREMENT WORK?

Chapter Two ...... page 15
   HOW DO YOU GET STARTED?

Chapter Three .... page 27
   HOW DO WE INCREASE THE BUSINESS?

Chapter Four ..... page 37
   THE IMPORTANCE OF GETTING REFERRALS

Chapter Five ...... page 49
   MANAGEMENT AND SYSTEMS FOR STAYING ON TOP

Chapter Six .... page 61
   WHAT TYPES OF PRODUCTS SHOULD BE USED?

Chapter Seven .... page 73
   COMPANY BENEFITS VERSUS PERSONAL BENEFITS

Chapter Eight ..... page 83
   THE IMPORTANCE OF MANAGING YOUR BASE

Chapter Nine ..... page 91
   HOW TO TRANSITION INTO A TEAM CONCEPT

Chapter Ten ..... page 101
   RUNNING A MATURE RETIREMENT BUSINESS

Chapter Eleven . page 109
   THIS KIND OF BUSINESS WILL CHANGE YOUR LIFE

FOREWORD

By definition, a secret is something that only a few people – if that many – are privy to. This book deals with a scenario that fits that definition, except with one very important difference: The masses are not excluded from having access to this "Secret." It's just that they have chosen not to listen to a persistent whisper that states, "Work with all the people," regardless of status, vocation or income level. They simply cannot – or will not – hear this whisper over the prevailing roar that declares, "Work only with the rich if you wish to be rich."

The result is that most financial professionals chase the same affluent clients, making success for them a very slippery slope at best. Meanwhile, the vast majority of the population comprises the other 95% of the people that are struggling to find someone they can pay to help them manage their funds and retire comfortably.

My hope is that by the end of this book you will be able to clearly hear the whisper, respond to it, and unlock the opportunity that this "secret" offers.

You will find that if you choose this path less-traveled, you will encounter less stress, work fewer hours and, paradoxically, feel more satisfied and fulfilled in every aspect of your occupation than you could have ever imagined possible.

Most importantly, you will find the answer to this question that I am asked so often by my peers: "What is your secret?" And when people start asking you the same question, you also will be able to answer your fellow financial professionals, with complete assurance, that "there is no secret!"

I trust as you read this book about how I have built my business that you will glean some things that will give you a strong edge in an otherwise very difficult business. Although my hope is that you will find this book to be highly motivational, in essence the goal is to provide you with a very straight-forward, practical instruction manual. As you read it, I'm confident you will take away ideas and strategies that you can implement immediately.

Before proceeding with this quest to teach you what I have learned over the past 15 years, it's important that I make one ac-knowledgement: I want to give all the credit to God for whatever good may come from this book. It was He who led me to this op-portunity, and He alone who created the ideas that have shaped my practice.

I think you will notice in the book's introduction that the cir-cumstances that brought me into this business are highly unusual. Since I was praying for a change in my working life, I was able to see God's hand in each initial step, just as well as I see it today. I refuse to claim any credit for the success of my practice, or the impact this book can have on your life, when I don't even manufac-ture the very air that I breathe that sustains my life. Now that this very crucial disclaimer is out of the way, we can begin!

INTRODUCTION

In December 1997, a series of successive events occurred that led to my becoming involved in the world of finance. I had recently changed companies and was suddenly in the position of having a 401(k) invested with a company that no longer employed me. Even though I was not a financial planner at that time, it seemed obvious to me that it would not be in my best interest to leave the funds under the management of the 401(k) provider of my former company.

I knew I needed to roll the funds into an Individual Retirement Account, so I began searching for a financial planner to help me accomplish this. As it turned out, this task was not as easy as it might sound. I apparently did not fit the "profile" of the client most financial professionals are looking for.

The financial planner who ultimately did my work actually did not seek me out and convince me to work with him. Instead, I sought *him* out and solicited *him* to help me move my funds. How often has that happened in the work that you do?

This experience forever changed my life, and I'm convinced that the knowledge of this process will change yours, too. It's a process that is repeated over and over every single day, thousands of times, as people leave companies they have been working for. They might be changing companies, retiring, or even getting laid off; whatever the reason, they may well find themselves in the same predicament I found myself in – looking for some solid financial advice and realizing that no one is looking for them!

As it happened, I had made a poor decision when I changed companies that year. I ended up in the most miserable job I had ever had, and certainly worked for the worst boss I had ever had.

I was working for the Tennessee Valley Authority as a manager at a nuclear power plant. On average I was working about 68 hours a week, and many times I was putting in more time than that. And this didn't even include time commuting to and from the plant.

Although I was grateful to have a steady job, I felt stuck. I had a child in college, along with the everyday expenses of our chosen lifestyle, so I needed the six-figure income I was earning. But there had to be more to life, I reasoned, than just work.

Frankly, I also missed my family. My wife and I were becoming strangers, and my children were growing up without having their father around. This frustration I felt became even more acute every Saturday morning as I again drove to work. I would pass the same house, probably two or three bedrooms, the home of a family I didn't know. But each day I would see the father out with his kids, either packing up their boat for a day at the lake, playing in the front yard on their "slip and slide," or throwing snowballs on snowy days.

When I drove home later that day, the boat would be back in their driveway. While I was laboring to do everything that nuclear power plant managers have to do to keep things running smoothly, this family had been out having a good time together and now they were already home, just "chilling" or doing whatever families did when their father wasn't chained to his job.

"I'd love to be him," I thought of the father, a man considerably younger than me whom I had frequently seen but had never actually met. One thing about him I did know: He obviously didn't have the pressing demands that I had to deal with 6-7 days a week.

One day I had a startling revelation, a moment of crystal-clear thinking: The only thing keeping me from being him – or at least being able to enjoy life as he did – was *me!*

So I began to think seriously about making a career change. The financial planner I had hired to take care of my 401(k) seemed to have a pretty good job. He appeared to be happy, successful, and he certainly didn't have to work hard to land my account.

So I decided to change careers and give myself a try at "financial planning." Admittedly, I hardly fit the mold of the person financial institutions are looking for – when was the last time you heard of a manager with an engineering background being aggressively recruited by an investment company or an insurance firm?

But I had formulated what I considered to be a reasonable plan. What I had in mind was that I would simply perform the same task that my financial planner had performed for me. That "task" became my business model, and people like me (those retiring or changing companies) were the profile of the client I sought out.

Admittedly, at the outset there were some challenges, but none that were impossible to overcome. A short four years later, my new career was providing me with an income that was more than ten times my former salary with the Tennessee Valley Authority in annual revenues, just by performing that same function over and over again.

Today, less than ten years from the time I started, the same activity has become the business plan for my investment group. During that span, our organization's profits have continued to grow exponentially year after year. I've won nearly every award that my company gives out, and I'm a member of the Million Dollar Round Table's Court of the Table and Top of the Table. If these accomplishments and the time it took to reach them seem unbelievable to you, join the club! It was just as startling to me. I entered this career without any idea this kind of result was possible.

I tell you this not to commend myself in any way, but merely to make an important point: Before starting as a financial planner, I had absolutely no background in sales, and did not have a degree in business or finance. People I consulted with as I embarked on this process were far from encouraging. In fact, I lost count of the times that people supposedly "in the know" told me categorically, "You will fail."

Yes, I was a poor candidate for this new career, except for one thing: I had discovered an important "secret." The secret was that there were – and still are – millions of people just like me preparing to retire or change companies, and they would be searching desperately for someone to help them relocate their retirement funds.

While most of the financial planning world chases the same business owner or high net-worth client, these other individuals are actually *seeking* someone willing to help them. In a sense, I had discovered the pretty girl that no one had asked to the dance. I didn't have the background to be a good fisherman, but partly because of my own experience, I had begun fishing where the fish were biting. And I was catching a whole pile of fish, while most of my peers with huddling around the same pond with empty hooks.

These individuals want and need your help. Statistically we know that the corporate work force is going to retire at least 50% of its employees over the next ten years, many of whom are major executives. The question is not whether the knowledge of this "secret" can turn someone's practice around. Rather, the question is: Will it turn *your* practice around? Are you *willing* to let it turn your practice around?

It doesn't matter if you've been in business for one year or forty years; whether you are a broker or an insurance professional, this platform can fit you. In many cases, as you know, financial professionals are hoping to turn over just the right rock one day and strike it big. *This is that rock!*

I never got into this business to make a lot of money. The only thing I coveted was the quality of life these guys had. No more work weeks of 68 hours or more, just the opportunity to earn a reasonable income and spend time with the people I loved the most – my wife and children.

What I discovered, almost unwittingly, was the "secret" – something that someone even with no background in this business could do with just desire. And in my case, that desire was fueled by picturing myself being back at the same miserable job, with the same long hours, that I had left behind. That in itself provided enough motivation for me to again reach for the phone and call somebody else who needed to know about what I had learned.

Should there be no desire on your part to expand and improve your practice, don't read this book! However, if that doesn't happen to be your situation, and you would be very pleased to make more money – and help some very needful people in the process – then if you read on and implement these principles, you will succeed!

If a simpleton like me – a success as a manager for TVA, but possessing no background in the things that experts say make for a good financial advisor – can succeed at this, I have no doubt that someone like you that already has experience in financial advising can and will succeed.

You will succeed not because you are that good – the author of this book certainly isn't – but you will succeed because *it's just that simple*. I wish you good luck after reading and implementing the ideas presented in this book. However, as I am convinced you will discover, *luck* is something you simply won't need!

Chapter One:

WHY SHOULD YOU DO RETIREMENT WORK?

There's a million dollars buried in your backyard!

Suppose someone were to come to you and inform you that there is a million dollars buried in your backyard and it's yours for the taking – no tricks, no strings attached. It's all yours, if you want it. If you really believed that statement, how would you approach getting your hands on it? Would you: *A)* Attend all kinds of seminars to determine just the right digging technique for reaching the million dollars? *B)* Go to every hardware center in the area to acquire just the right tools to excavate the million dollars? Or *C) Just dig it up?*

This might seem like a silly illustration, but it's a great entry point for getting into the heart of this book: Why should you, as a financial professional, do retirement planning? The reason, as I've stated above in the title of this chapter, is because if you decide to work in this area, there *is* a million dollars buried in your backyard!

Just to set the stage, let me explain that retirement planning in my practice consists primarily of advising individuals that work for large corporations and are approaching or starting their retirement years. This individual typically averages $60,000-70,000 in total income per year. It's important for you to know this from the outset, because this is in contrast to the high net-worth client who may own his or her corporation.

Let me clarify exactly what we do just a little bit more. We are not talking about marketing 401(k)'s or 403(b)'s. What we *are* talking about is rolling these funds away from the company fund manager. This is the function that can and will produce the millions that, unbeknownst to most financial professionals, are hidden in your backyard. That being said, I think it's safe to move on.

I hope we didn't lose your interest by explaining the kind of work we are talking about doing. If you are still with us at this point, we have successfully made it past the first hurdle, but there are many more yet to come.

Any established financial professional, or even a new trainee, understandably is going to have some very valid questions concerning whether they should approach this work as we have defined it:

- *How about competition? Is there going to be a lot of it? If so, I might not want to face this issue.*

- *What about training? Am I going to need a lot of new training?*

- *How about my goal to impact society in a positive way? Will this help the world to be a better place because I performed this work?*

- *How easy will it be to grow my base of clients using this practice model? What about the target market? How good is it?*

- *What is the risk of my business failing if I implement this process?*

- *What percentage of wallet share can I expect from the average client?*

- *What effect does gender have on this market? (If you are a female financial professional, this would probably be your first question.)*

- *What about age? "I'm just out of college." Or, "Am I too old to change my practice?"*

- *Finally, how long does it take me to put this process in place and make it work?*

These are a lot of questions to answer, but each is well worth considering. Let's get started, so you can start digging up the million dollars.

How about competition?

Let's begin by discussing the all-important subject of competition. It's the thing most people fear in any business, and in this arena, there is almost none. Companies offer **_generalized_** benefits for the employee, while you, on the other hand, offer **_personalized_** benefits. The 401(k) provider is not interested in your potential client; they are interested in the company he or she works for. Conversely, in your role as a financial professional, you are not at all interested in the company the individual works for; you are interested in your potential client. If this is your competition, then you have won before the game has even started!

Compare this to fighting in the dog-eat-dog world of chasing the high net-worth client where the competition is almost insane. If you've done this before, you know the months of work it often takes even to get an audience with a lower level assistant, who often screens out professionals without giving them a chance. The question begs asking: Would you rather swim against the current, or with the current? Believe me – there is almost no competition in the retirement planning world.

What about training? Am I going to need more?

Training is another issue that scares us in the business world. I don't want to leave anyone with the impression that education is not important, but most of the time with retirement work, you will be "competing" with someone who works as a benefits specialist for a particular company. They are hourly employees and have little or no training as a financial professional. They don't understand the concept of using life insurance to maximize a pension because they are not in the business of explaining options to the company plan. They simply explain how the company benefits work.

You already are very well trained in comparison to the human resource employee, your primary "competitor." You are able to answer many questions covering a broad range. Occasionally, you might have to compete with another financial professional for retirement work, but that is rare. Most financial professionals frankly are not seeking to do this work.

I want to pose a question that relates to the area of training. Do you remember the million-dollar example at the beginning of the chapter – that pile of money buried just below the surface in your backyard that you're walking over or past every day, never knowing it's there? The reason you won't need a more broad-based training is because you aren't dealing with multiple issues – *it's just one backyard, one million dollars*. It's very specialized, and so is your training.

Unless you find yourself competing against another retirement specialist, you are far better trained than most financial professionals. I know this might sound like the height of sarcasm, but it is a fact – there is a lot more than a million dollars buried in your backyard if we are talking about retirement planning, and you currently possess all the tools necessary to do the work if you are a trained financial professional!

You may not have worked in this area before, but why wouldn't you want to get a piece of something this simple?

How about my goal to impact society in a positive way?

You might now be wondering if this type of work provides a service that is needed by society. This is where things really begin to get interesting – what I have found most compelling of all.

In my opinion, there is no area so desperately lacking in advice than that of the individual retiring from his company as his career draws to an end. Will he have enough money to last him until he dies? Will his spouse be okay after he's gone? How much should he spend? What about estate planning?

He can't get this advice from the 401(k) provider. They aren't in the business of helping the individual with these sorts of things, and in some cases, they are actually *prohibited* from advising in those areas. The benefits group is there to explain the benefits, not to provide *individual financial counseling*. So if you want to make your mark on society, you might have just located your divine calling!

Contrast this to the advisor pursuing the high net-worth client who hangs up on three potential advisors before he's finished his first cup of coffee in the morning. Where are you really needed? It's almost a silly question at this point. Perhaps a more meaningful question would be: Why would you want to work on anything else? And by the way, folks, we are just getting warmed up!

Too often we're caught up in the never-ending, often futile pursuit of Mr. High Net Worth. Meanwhile, the prospective retiree is languishing through the ordeal of trying to figure out if they should use option A, B or C, and at the same time trying to develop some type of spreadsheet that will tell him how long his money will last.

These individuals don't have any idea how to proceed at this point, but you do! You are totally prepared to answer these kinds of questions. You really wanted to do the same thing for the millionaire who hung up on you last week, totally disinterested. But new retirees are *actually looking* for someone to explain it to them.

Are you beginning to see the picture? The difference is startling. You think you need the high net-worth client, but he doesn't seem to be interested in you. On the other hand, the prospective retirees know they need help with their decisions. If by chance at this point you're still convinced it's more profitable to chase the guy who doesn't want to be caught, go back and read the introduction to this book again!

These people – new and prospective retirees – need everything you're peddling, and they know it: investment advice, life insurance, in some cases health insurance, as well as long-term care insurance. And they are certainly interested in estate planning, because they're not as young as they once were.

The most wonderful part of all this, however, is that many of them have never had an opportunity to work with a financial professional because they have worked for a corporation for 30 years or more. The business owner may think you are a pest, but these folks typically think you are brilliant – and compared to what they have dealt with at their company, you are!

How easy will it be to grow my base of clients using this practice model?

Let's look next at where you go from that first piece of retirement work you do. How do you grow your client base? That initial client isn't the end of the road; it's really the beginning. Before your new client – let's call him Joe – leaves the company, he begins talking about you to all his co-workers. Joe tells them how helpful you've been and how you advised him regarding his 401(k). The water cooler talks are now about you and what you can do for them, and soon you will be helping some of Joe's co-workers with their own retirement choices.

Additionally, the adult children of this new client need to be introduced to you because they will inherit the money when your client is gone. Allow me to provide an example that illustrates this in my practice. I had a client who retired from a local company a few years ago. My team and I performed updates and met all service requests from this gentleman. We established a valuable relationship with him. He was our friend.

Unfortunately, he passed away about five years after his retirement. We had taken care of setting up a trust for him and doing some estate planning, and suddenly there were two grown children that were the recipients of his estate. We had met one of them during our frequent visits to see our client in the hospital. We had already formed a relationship with her, so it was no surprise to us when she asked us to help her in establishing accounts to receive her share of the proceeds.

We had never met the other adult child, who as it turned out was a physician at a hospital in another state. When we did meet him, because of the care we had shown to his father, the son reinvested his share of the proceeds with us. That was hardly the end of it. As a result of our connection with the son, we have now done investment work for several of the other doctors at the hospital where he performs his medical practice.

All of this work was made possible simply because my client's son valued the help we had given his dad. By the time I finished working with the additional doctors, I had invested more than ten times the amount the original client had left behind in his estate.

Scenarios like this are hardly unique. Your newly retired client might have parents who are still living. They may have a need for a financial professional too, because they probably retired without anyone helping them. If you've provided their son or daughter with good investment assistance, wouldn't they be inclined to work with you as well?

How about the target market?

Hopefully you are starting to see things more clearly now, but we are still only touching the hem of the garment. Because of the huge throng of Baby Boomers marching toward retirement, the largest target market in the world is potentially standing right at your doorstep. Every aspect of society has profited from their existence and catered to them.

An important thing to keep in mind is the industries that pursued this generation as customers didn't just sell diapers for the business owners' kids; they sold them to everyone, regardless of income level. So why would we, as financial professionals, only target a small percentage of the Boomers? Why should we target just the wealthy ones? If we fail to service the employees of the big corporation, the people whose years of dedicated labor helped to line the pockets of the wealthy corporate leaders, we will have missed the biggest prize of all, not to mention the fact that it was the easiest apple to pick.

Just as people tell all their friends about the new car they took for a test drive or the great TV they just bought, they will tell all of them about you when you have successfully addressed their retirement needs. You're the person who knew their company benefits better than their benefits manager did; you understood investments better than their 401(k) provider; and you realized that choices on amounts of pension levels for leaving a bene-fit to a loved one were nothing more than a cheap imitation of life insurance.

The vast majority of these emerging retirees aren't buying the stuff on television that says they should do it themselves. Most don't build their own houses, change their own oil, or wash their own cars. They certainly aren't interested in expending all their energy and effort trying to reach retirement, only to discover they have to become a financial advisor when they get there!

Don't mislead yourself by thinking they probably don't need or want you. They just haven't found you yet! How about making yourself available? If you do, it will change at least two lives – yours and theirs.

What is the risk of my business failing if I implement this process?

Keeping your practice afloat is always a concern because we all know we're going to miss one every now and then, regardless of how good we are or how hard we try! The niche market I am describing is not totally rejection-free, but it is worry-free.

Let me explain: Financial professionals often spend days, weeks, even months putting together the perfect proposals for a business owner. In spite of all this work, they might lose the case they've spent all that time on to another firm. This can be devas-tating to the professional's practice. So let's contrast this pursuit of the small business owner with the target market for my firm.

We have had months when we worked with large groups of peo-ple that were leaving a particular company. This happens more often than you would imagine as companies downsize, offer early-outs, or sell out. Here's a common scenario: Let's say that out of forty-five employees leaving a particular company, we only did retirement work for fifteen of them. Based on that proportion, we only batted in the .300s, speaking in baseball terms. (But if you understand baseball, batting over .300 is still good.) Because we were working a number of different clients, rather than hoping to catch a single big fish, my firm experienced phenomenal profits that month.

In case I haven't made this concept clear, by taking this approach the loss of one potential client will never disastrously affect my practice. To use another metaphor, there are so many birds to shoot at, you're bound to hit a lot of them – you will eat well! You won't worry what you could have said or done differently with one crucial potential client because you didn't place all of your eggs in one basket. One individual case will not make or break you.

What percentage of wallet share can I expect from the average client?

What about the very important consideration of wallet share? Most millionaires have several planners, and each is just trying to hang onto his share. By comparison, the individual with the $500,000 rollover from their old company has only one person: you. We will talk about diversification techniques in future chapters, but for now, understand you are their only planner. You are the one who will do their life insurance, long-term care, grandkids' college funds, etc. You are it!

I understand the other side because I've been involved in it. I do have several high net-worth clients who think we hung the moon! But we only own about 30% of their business. However, for those clients who don't run a business and are worth less than about $1.5 million, we own approximately 85% of their wallet share, on average.

Also, did I mention that trying to hang on to the high net-worth client is a slippery slope at best? But to the other guy, you were there when no one else cared, and he won't leave you. Clients like these will be with you ten or twenty years from now, and you will have the satisfaction of handing a check to their wife or adult children when they are gone, having served a husband

and father by playing a part in his family's financial security well into the future.

What effect does gender have on this market?

As I mentioned earlier, if you are a female financial professional reading this book, understandably you might be wondering if this type of work is for you. Actually, I hope you *are* wondering that because the last sentence in the previous section applies directly to you.

My firm works with many widows. Face it guys, on average wives simply outlive us. That being the case, do you think that widow would rather work with a male or female financial professional?

The prospective retirees are looking for help, and even if they are male, they want to work with someone who cares about them, as well as someone that their wife is comfortable with. The high net-worth male business owner, on the other hand, often does carry a gender bias. He thinks (and I apologize for having to say this, ladies, but it's reality) that you don't understand how to run a business.

For the company employee, however, gender bias is actually reversed. The company employee thinks that as a female, you know all about budgeting and running a household, issues that they are now facing. The male might make a decision on which car he will buy without his wife's input, but that is not true of his decision about whom they should use as a financial professional to manage their retirement.

The evidence of this fact has been played out over and over again in my office. For all intents and purposes, the husband is talking, but his wife is the decision-maker. Many men assume they will be the first to go, so it's natural they want to work with someone their wife feels comfortable with.

I have a good friend who is doing retirement planning in another state. She works with a lot of utility company retirees.

Most of her clients are men, but their wives love her and they are instrumental in creating her referral base.

What about my age?

How about your age? This is another reasonable question to ask. You're simply too young to make it in this niche market, right? Wrong again. The high net-worth client usually won't give you an audience, but the people we are talking about will, and there are many reasons for this.

We might have worn this principle out by now, I know, but the fact is, *beggars can't be choosers* – and you were there when they needed you. They will use you. It won't be any problem for you to get the meeting. The big reason, however, relates to the contrasting needs. The business owner is working with people who are helping him take care of things **now**. He or she is not usually looking very far into the future. The prospective retiree, however, is looking at someone that will work with his family until he dies – and beyond. I think you can quickly pick up on what this implies – in this case, younger can be a distinct advantage.

I have had many clients who are not much older than I am that have looked me in the eye and asked about who will take over my practice when I retire. That's why it's a comfort to me to have my sons working with my firm, and also why the team concept is so important to my firm. In essence, the client wants someone who has gray hair, representing experience, but also has the longevity of a 29-year-old. Last time I checked, you can't do that in one body.

So if you're a fairly young person in this industry, your age can give you a marketable, competitive advantage over the distinguished financial professional in this market. The prospective or recent retiree needs your youth. In the case of the high net-worth client, he doesn't. Age, in most cases, falls in the deficit column if you are approaching the high net-worth client. But it's a big plus in my line of work.

How long does it take to implement this process and make it work in my practice?

The last objection that may be concerning you is this: How much time will it require to get a new practice off the ground, or in the case of the experienced financial professional, how long will it take to implement the new principles? This might be your most compelling reason of all for taking a serious look at this niche market.

Those of you who have been in this business for years understand – painfully so – the operative adage of *"good things come to those who wait."* I have often heard my colleagues that don't work in niche markets indicate they just finished a case that was five years in the making. The prospective retiree, on the other hand, sometimes receives an early out package that they didn't see coming. They might actually have only weeks to make the decision on what they will do with these funds, including their severance pay, so the last thing they are interested in is having to wait.

This means your practice could, and in many cases would, receive payment for work you do within days or weeks. Let's see: *A)* You work diligently for five years and finally get paid for all the time you spent, if you can survive that long; or *B)* you work with someone and get paid your commissions in a very reasonable time frame. Which one do you want?

This market, if implemented correctly, shows immediate results. The example of a fisherman works well here. Do you want to fish for five years in hopes of catching one big fish, or fish in a large school of smaller fish where you catch one every cast? Sometimes the difference in success and failure of a practice is *three years.*

The example of schooling fish is a good one. But I can think of one even better than that. Do you remember the old commercial for Lay's potato chips: "Betcha can't eat just one?" With retirees, you won't usually get just one. Hey, I would be willing to bet you can't sign *just one!* I have never heard any of my colleagues who worked five years to get a big case indicate that they got ten more at the same time. Whether you are just starting in this profession or looking for something to expand your mature practice, this is it!

Does any of this appeal to you? You can fit this practice into any situation. There are no objections by the financial professional that can stand against the world of opportunity in this niche market. Whether old or young, male or female, new practice or old practice, educated to the gills or yet to be fully trained, a person owing a debt to society or someone just wanting to be more comfortable financially, this works for you. And for the experienced professionals that want to put their practice in a good position so they don't have to work as hard in five years, this is what you have been looking for.

This market will allow you to annuitize your business so you can predict with uncanny accuracy what you will earn in January five years from now if all you do is simply turn the lights on. Do you want a business where your kids, your wife, or your cousin can be part of it? Do you want to build a legacy? This can become your foundation.

Do you want something where you can start by calling prospects and end with them calling you? No more hunting – you just found it! Do you want to be able to move to the mountains, or to the coast, and take your business with you? You can: I understand there are folks retiring in both of those areas. This concept simply meets or exceeds all dreams and expectations, if you just answer just one question correctly: Do you want to do this?

That might sound like a silly question, but some professionals feel this niche market isn't for them. They are and always have been trout fishermen, and they don't want to fish for bass, even if they are schooling. You know what? That's okay. That's why God made us all different. However, for those that don't fall in the category of either being unwilling or not wanting to change, we are going to have a great time – and your life will never be the same again.

You are about to become the person you only dreamed about. You're going to have the financial security you've always imagined, take the vacations you've only read about, and make the lives of your loved ones match the books you've read that describe great family lifestyles. Not only that, but you will also touch the lives of people you have yet to meet – in a very positive way. This world will be better because you were here.

Sacrifice is what those not in your inner circle will think caused it, but *sacrifice* is a word you're going to eliminate from your vocabulary. The reason is very simple: The results are not determined by how hard you work at the business; rather, they are governed by *how you do this business.* Simply put yourself in the right position with the right companies and establish a referral base, and you can seize the future.

Does this sound even remotely like the way you had visualized your business? If so, let's move from **dreaming** *to* **living the dream.**

You are going to see that the "secret" to success in this market is that **there is no secret.** Getting back to the metaphor we used at the beginning of this chapter, *there is a million dollars buried just below the surface in your backyard.* You and I are going to work together as we cover the following chapters, but *you and you alone are going to dig it up!*

Chapter Two:

HOW DO YOU GET STARTED?

Don't spend another night with the frogs!

There is a curious passage in the Old Testament of the Bible, found in the book of Exodus. The stage is set after God has sent frogs as one of the plagues to force the mighty pharaoh of Egypt to set the Israelites free after 400 years of captivity. There are frogs everywhere – in the food and cooking utensils, every room and closet, everywhere you step. Already reeling from the earlier plagues, Pharaoh has had enough, so he calls on Moses and Aaron to get rid of the frogs.

This time, unlike with the previous plagues the Lord has sent, Moses doesn't immediately call on God to eliminate the plague. Instead, he addresses Pharaoh in Exodus 8:9 and says, "I leave to you the honor of setting the time for me to pray for you, your officials, and your people that you and your houses may be rid of the frogs, except for those that will remain in the Nile." In verse 10, we read Pharaoh's amazing answer: "Tomorrow"!

He knew how to rectify the problem and escape the misery, and yet he still says, "tomorrow." Why in the world did he want to spend another night with the frogs! The reason I offer this biblical example is my hope that this won't be your answer once you know how to turn your business around. Let's hope you will decide to do it *right now*.

How do you get 'in' with a company?

The question I have been asked more than any other is, "How does someone get 'in' with a company?" In other words, how did I succeed in getting to the point where I have 100 or more clients from a particular company that all used me to do their retirement rollovers? How did I get started with each company?

It's really not difficult at all, but it's probably not what you are thinking – and there are more ways than one to do it. Let's get started, beginning with the scenario of a financial professional who already has an established practice. (Be patient: We'll address those of you who don't fit this profile next.)

Let's say you're that professional, and you have somewhere between 200 and 600 clients. Your first step is to find people already in your book of business who work for large companies. Examples of this could be phone companies, the local power company, manufacturing plants, auto dealerships, hospitals, grocery store chains, large real estate firms, etc. Most of these people will retire at some point – and as we've already said, they'll need the help of someone like you.

Your next move would be to call your client in for a meeting. Your client may be nearing retirement age, in which case you are ready to help them with their retirement planning. But if they haven't quite reached the age to retire yet, there still might be an opportunity to do some work for them because hundreds of companies offer in-service withdrawal features from their 401(k)'s. This means the employee doesn't even have to reach retirement age to have control over part of their money.

With just a little bit of research, you can determine which companies in your client book have an in-service withdrawal feature. Many times the employees aren't aware of this benefit. Most of the companies offering in-service withdrawals allow approximately 95% of the funds to be removed if the employee is 60 or older. When you explain this to the employee, it will be eye-opening to them that you know more about their 401(k) than their human resources director does.

At this point, many of your clients having this feature available will be ready to act. However, if they are unsure about whether or not they want to take advantage of this newly found freedom, the first question to ask is whether they think the 401(k) provider is more interested in *them* or the *company* they work for. I'm certain they can answer that question quickly enough. In contrast, you, the financial professional, have no interest whatsoever in the company your client works for. Your interest is solely in them.

Comparing available funding options

The second question to ask is how many fund choices does their 401(k) provider offer for their investment? Many times there are fewer than ten funds to choose from; you, the financial professional, have unlimited fund options. It's easy to see which way the future looks brighter.

We don't intend to belabor this point, but simply to make it clearer, consider the following example: If you were playing golf with a friend who was your equal in ability, but he had a bag of clubs to choose from while you only had one club to use, who do you think would win? Additionally, it should be pointed out that the tax treatment of a 401(k) is completely different than that of an IRA. If the employee and their spouse were to be tragically killed while the money is in the 401(k), the distribution to their heirs would be taxable. 401(k)'s are not inheritable. IRAs on the other hand, can be passed to a spouse, a child, or a relative with the taxes being deferred.

That's probably enough in the way of questions to seal the deal, but if it's not, we will talk about some other helpful questions later in this chapter.

The process from this point, however, is a simple one. I am sure that given the opportunity, you have a product ready to house their 401(k) and roll it into an IRA. This process can usually be done on the telephone in just minutes. If that isn't the case, the paperwork can be obtained either from the company you are transferring the funds from or from the new trustee.

This process for the new agent is the same as we promised earlier. You undoubtedly are acquainted with prospects that work for large companies, and this would be the best place to begin your new business. Set appointments with those who are nearing retirement age or those who have in-service withdrawal options. If you are just starting out, it is advisable to team up with an agent who is experienced. Even though you will be sharing your commission, you will have a much better chance of getting the case if you are working with an agent with experience in this type of transaction.

You might also want to look for an experienced agent who has not performed this kind of work. You would be able to offer them your help on their "B" and "C" type clients. These clients, who are not the top tier for this agent, can be the start of a retirement base. The combination of your new, fresh perspective and the existing agent's second tier of clients can result in a major transformation for both of you.

Relying on clients, not HR people

There is a myth that says you should start this process by going to the human resources director of a company and that they will lead you to all the employees. In my years of experience, let me tell you what I have learned: *That just doesn't work*! The HR people already have a job to do, and helping you to do yours isn't part of it.

On the other hand, the process we've just described will work again and again because once you have done it, the new client will tell others he works with about what a good thing they've found, and you will be on your way! This fact-finding expedition also locks in other crucial information, such as when they are expecting to leave the company for good and, in case you are working an in-service withdrawal, when the rest of their money will become available for you to manage.

It's a perfect time to ask your client, "Who do you know that can benefit from this newfound knowledge?" It takes a little while, but at some point you will have so many clients that you will be able to establish a *retirement matrix* that will predict with perfect accuracy your business future. The retirement matrix is simply a record of each client telling you when they plan to leave their company. In this matrix, you place their names, along with the amount of their available funds in the month and year that they will retire.

You would want to duplicate this process with as many companies as you can think of so you can grow your referral base. There are no limitations of any kind.

What about the 'lump sum benefit'?

In many cases, these same companies also provide a lump sum benefit. These monies are not available until the employee retires. They are established by a rule of 70 or 80, which equates simply to age plus years of service. However, a little-known fact is that just because the employee stays longer, it does not mean the lump sum will be bigger. The total figure of the lump sum is affected by a multiplier, and to quote Ebenezer Scrooge from Charles Dickens' *A Christmas Carol*, "almost any little thing can affect it."

You are the person that will help the prospective retirees realize this. You will also help them begin to see what the lump sum looks like if they were to retire tomorrow, remove the funds, and start to live off of them at a certain point – let's say, 60 years of age. We don't want to create undo stress, but in today's environment, it is worth mentioning that if the company goes bankrupt, this money could very well go from $600,000 to zero in nothing flat!

The monies being removed and invested prior to such a destructive event would insure that none of their retirement would be lost. The figures can usually be obtained from their pension center, and if your clients have the figures projected into the future and have the company multiplier changed, they will begin to see why it is important to visit with you.

Here's a quick example: Employee "A" from the power company has 80 points of service (years + age) and the multiplier was 4 – a total of $320,000. He or she naturally thought that if they stayed for one more year they would have more money. But the company multiplier changes in six months to 3. Let's do it again: 81 points (we added in the extra year) multiplied by 3 equals $243,000. They actually *lost* $87,000 by working one year longer!

You don't have to be a rocket scientist to help them understand the impact of this. You are simply using printed information that they hadn't looked at before to help them understand their own vulnerability. This isn't much different than a coach talking to an aging player about his future financially if he keeps playing.

When opportunity knocks, answer the door!

As you can imagine, by providing this vital information you have just become a valued asset to this client, and that word gets around fast. You could pick up the newspaper and find out that a company with a defined benefit plan (i.e., a lump sum provision) was having an early-out offering. Even if this was not a company you had worked with in the past, after acquiring a name and phone number of one of the employees, you could reference them to some other companies whose employees you have helped with this issue. You become a valuable resource to help them decide whether or not to take the early out.

The average size of one of these rollovers, in my book of business, is around $500,000. If you get ten of them, well, you can do the math! The question we come back to again is, "How do I get the names and phone numbers?" When you're dealing with a potential total commission range of somewhere between $50,000 and $150,000, you'll ask anyone – your cousin, uncle, best friend, neighbor, or whoever you can find, until you get the name of someone who works there. It's just like the million dollars in the backyard we've been talking about – *dig it up!*

I think you are beginning to see the techniques, and we are just starting to open the doors. There are many, many more.

Examining who really benefits

One such door is the one that confronts the client with a pension fund. He or she has to navigate a myriad of options their company presents to them. The options involve his or her premature death. Here is where the life insurance professional comes in. What would you call a concept where you pay a premium now, and the company pays the beneficiary when you die? That's right, you'd call it life insurance. The company, however, doesn't. It refers to it as options A-E, and none of these options even remotely make sense to the poor, bewildered employee.

They only know that they are committed to taking proper care of their spouse who has been with them for all of their life. The company plan is not prepared to take care of anyone's death other than that of the employee. The plan is built on the premise that the employee gives up part of his or her pension dollars to give a portion of the benefit to a surviving spouse. If the employee's spouse should die before him, or if both the employee and spouse die simultaneously, the program simply does not work, and the employee has wasted years of pension dollars.

This whole concept is very familiar to insurance professionals, known as "pension maximization." In case this isn't your area of expertise, this is where you might want to team up with the insurance professional if you have already gained the retiree's trust through rolling their 401(k). If you are an insurance professional and you have started with the client at the pension maximization process, then you'll want to team with an investment professional to roll the client's 401(k). Should you be a firm that does both, I don't need to give you any further advice.

Which is better: Irrevocable, or changeable?

We have to make it clear that whatever involvement and expertise you have in this part of the retirement decision, *the person making the decision needs you.* They can do nothing but lose out if they choose the company's plan for leaving money to a spouse at their death.

The prospective client didn't work for thirty or forty years so they could leave a part of their pension to the company they worked for.

There is no alternative offered in the company plan. Let's look at the insurance alternatives. If the employee's financial situation changes – perhaps they inherit a large sum of money – the company plan is irrevocable. Your plan, on the other hand, is changeable. Death benefits can be lowered, thus reducing the insurance premium, or it can be cancelled altogether, and the money returned to the employee.

The reason the insurance plan is called pension maximization is because the employee is now in control of the process, not the company they were working for. The adult children can pay the premium if the prospect no longer needs the insurance, and the beneficiaries can be the grandchildren. The beneficiary could also be the individual's favorite charity. The combinations are endless, and the choice of what to do with the money is totally in the control of the employee.

When we use the company plan, the pension benefit in many cases is completely lost. When you use the pension maximization plan with life insurance, the pension can never be lost. It will always go to someone the employee loves. And in all honesty, I don't believe that will ever be the company they were working for. The employee has earned it; why shouldn't he or she do with it as they wish?

Look at it this way: As Americans, we are used to making decisions about what to do with the income we have earned. You would never buy a car from a dealership that informed you a stripped-down version of a car was the only choice you had in a make of automobile. You want options: clocks, stereos, DVD players, heated seats, etc. You want these options available, even if you don't choose them. Your prospective client wants the same kind of options with their retirement.

When they find out that their company only sells a stripped-down version of retirement, but you offer the equal to heated seats, they will buy from you, even if they have to pay more to get some of these options. That's just the way Americans are wired. They will buy from you even if they don't take many of the options that weren't available from their company. They will buy simply because you offer them choices. When it comes to using our money, we want choices. These same people will frequent a restaurant that has a large selection, even if they purchase the same entrée every time. *We like and want choices.*

There are many cases that we can find on file where society was benefited because the pension monies were directed to a deserving cause rather than dying with the employee. So whether the proceeds go to family, friends, or a worthy cause the employees believe in, you are making yourself valuable at this point, not only to your prospect but also to everything within their reach. You gave them the gift of the Midas touch when it comes to their pension.

Once they understand this process, it's a no-brainer. You've earned a big place in the future of their children because you, not the company, were able to show how to pass the pension on. And this involved being able to make choices.

Problems with 'Option A'

The most popular choice offered by most companies is Option A, or a 100% survivor benefit. This option allows the company to keep about $500 a month from a $3,000 a month pension, in exchange for a spousal benefit. The employee who selects this benefit will receive a lower amount of $2,500 a month, but in exchange the company promises to continue to pay the same pension to the employee's spouse after the death of the employee.

But what if the employee's spouse dies first? *The benefit is lost.* The employee gave up $500 a month *for a spouse who is no longer living.* Company benefits, once chosen, are irrevocable. Your plan, on the other hand is tailored to meet the needs of the client; it is not a one-size-fits-all plan like the company plan.

With you, the employee owns his own pension, and now you have allowed them to take control of things. They can take care of their spouse in whatever fashion fits them. For the same $500 that they would have given up under Option A, they can now purchase life insurance, which could provide an even better pension for their spouse. And should the spouse die first, the life insurance is simply cancelled, unlike the irrevocable company plan. At any rate, there will be a variety of choices for the employee who works with you, rather than having to take the company plan.

Helping them understand the details

There are a couple of other minor fine points about pension benefits that are worthy of note. Company benefits are taxable; death proceeds are not. Pension benefits are not flexible; insurance benefits are as flexible as Stretch Armstrong (remember that silly little play toy?) Pension benefits die with you; life insurance starts at your death. The list can go on and on.

You, the financial professional, are the catalyst that makes the pension work. They need you, and when you have helped them, that's a message they will pass on to their friends. Are you beginning to see the picture? This concept of working with retirees is multi-generational – and the growth of your business can become geometric.

What about the individual who is trying to decide on the concept of level-income Social Security? This concept simply means choosing to get the Social Security benefits now in exchange for lowering the company pension at age 62. Now there's a concept that almost everyone was taught in school, right? Maybe their company, let's call it the ABC Electric Company, offered courses on how to figure this concept out. Don't kid yourself. *It just simply didn't happen.*

So prospective retirees, many of them without a clue in this area, need someone like you to help them understand it – and they will tell all their friends how important you were to their retirement when you do. You have been trained for just this kind of exercise. The employee who is younger than 59½ is able to delay drawing from their IRA and avoid paying a 10% penalty. The employee avoids paying all kinds of taxes because of your understanding of this concept.

The employee simply takes the extra pension money offered by the company until age 62. The pension then lowers, and now they have to fill in the gap with IRA money, but they no longer have the worry of paying the extra 10% tax penalty because they are past age 60. The client using this concept saves countless dollars in tax revenue, and in many cases, it allows them to take the early-out package. They wanted to take the package all along, but probably wouldn't have been able to without your help.

Paralyzed by what they don't know

Retirees are afraid to do things they don't understand, and they don't understand Level Income Social Security. The decision isn't always this clear cut, and that's the other reason why they need you. There are cases where the individuals have other monies that are not 401(k) or IRA money, so in that scenario it might be worthwhile to keep their pension stable even after Social Security starts. This would secure a bigger increase in monthly monies when Social Security payments begin.

There are many variables that affect the choice of whether or not to accept the company's offer of early Social Security through the level income plan. These choices are affected by the employee's age and the tax treatment of the funds the employee has to use at retirement. The way it gets done, and the decision tree that accomplishes it, are not the issue. The issue is simply that they need help to figure it out for their greatest advantage.

You haven't talked to them in this area about any product or item that will earn you money. But the information you provided was vital for their retirement. You didn't earn any commissions – but you earned their trust. That will create commissions in the future, not just from the prospect but from many of their friends as well. You will be creating more referrals in the process of helping out in areas that won't pay you. This is one of many concepts that will continue to build your base of prospects.

These concepts we have mentioned are door openers, and you possess – either on your own or by teaming with other individuals – the ability to win their business. You simply have to pick up the phone and find someone that you can explain it to. We will discuss in future chapters how to build on your referral base so you don't have to "cold call" nearly as much.

But the issue now at hand is not how to *increase* your base of retirees, but rather how to *get* a base of retirees. The concepts we have reviewed will work. The burning question is: *Will you?* You won't fail if you get prospects in the office and use your newly found knowledge to help them. They won't pick up the phone, however, and beg you to demonstrate how much better you can make their life after they retire. You must take the initiative and call them.

You wouldn't be in this business if you hadn't already prospected clients. So you understand that the future is what you decide to make it.

The question is essentially the same as the one that Moses posed to Pharaoh. When do you want to make your life much better than it has been? When do you want to move from mundane to magical? When would you like to make the change? Today, tomorrow, or six months from now?

Take my advice:

Don't make Pharaoh's mistake. Don't spend another night with the frogs!

Chapter Three:

HOW DO WE INCREASE THE BUSINESS?

Good news really does travel fast!

My past occupation, which as I explained earlier indirectly led to my new career, was serving in a management capacity with the Tennessee Valley Authority. During my years there, I often had the opportunity to see firsthand how much time that individuals would spend drinking coffee and talking about their impending retirement. The only difference then was that I had to answer for their behavior concerning the amount of work that was getting done – or *not* getting done. On more than one occasion I had to remind the "coffee break" crowd that if they didn't break it up, their retirement might come sooner than they anticipated!

These little "coffee break" gatherings seemed to always have a leader, or at least someone who was guiding the discussions. They would enumerate with great pride the information they had become privy too. There was always much discussion about the professional organizations the individual had sought counsel from.

Therein lies the secret you need for increasing your retirement business. These individuals were the mouthpieces for their respective financial professionals. They enjoyed sharing their experience and telling what they'd learned. As I listened to these informative individuals, they often reminded me of birds. They say it's impossible to make a blackbird talk. And it's just as impossible to make a parrot *stop* talking.

These individuals are "parrots," and while you won't find many of them in a crowd of future retirees, you don't need many of them to increase your business. They can grow a business more quickly than a wildfire spreads in a dense forest, and it's their natural instinct to do so.

Concentrating initially on one company

As you get started, it's best to single out one company, like DuPont for example, to launch your retirement business. You want to gain entrance into other companies similar to the one you use for getting started so you can gain a regular flow of commissions. The "retirement parrot" will help you accomplish this task. I'm not speaking disparagingly about them, but the reality is this: They feel it is their God-given responsibility to get you an audience with as many people as possible. If, in the quest to help you get in front of prospects from other companies, the parrot introduces you to a person just like them (another parrot) at the new company, then the opportunities are limitless.

The prospects-turned-clients within these companies hold the keys to your future in this business. Your meetings with them should take place often enough that they can realize how much you value the help they are providing. You are genuinely grateful for their efforts, and you want to continue a dialogue with them about the work you're doing together.

Certainly not every client is a parrot, but all new clients can be utilized to gain referrals. Most new clients will be willing to provide referrals in some manner – it could be anything from names of friends and family members to actually offering up a copy of their company directory!

Once you have at least one parrot identified, you now have possession of the financial planning equivalent of a missile launcher; your position – along with your retirement business – will begin to explode. You can see your positive outcome almost assured if you can succeed in getting one of your clients to list the birthdays and ages (or at least approximations) of the employees in the directory. Armed with the ages of the prospects, you become almost unstoppable – this will be true no matter how strong (or poor) your interpersonal skills are.

Confirming the contract

Reviewing the new contract with the client is very important. Not only do you want to make sure they have no misgivings about their recent investment; it also gives you another opportunity to get in front of your client in the hope that they will refer you to others who are leaving the same employer.

The greatest treasure you can discover is the client that is still working for a company but took an in-service withdrawal from their 401(k). You now have an individual who is still serving the employer but is already your client. It would be even better if they were parrots, but whether that is the case or not, they will be very important to growing your practice.

It only takes a few of these individuals to get you going. Unlike the retiree who is trying to help you grow your practice but is no longer in contact with the employees in the plant, these individuals have inside knowledge of layoffs, retirements and deaths. These issues all require your assistance. There is only one of you, but these individuals can and will multiply your presence many times over.

We don't want to forget that on top of all the doors this new client can open for you, they are still working, so most of their money remains in the 401(k). You will now be able to run a retirement module to help them decide on their retirement date. Place that date and the commissions associated with their retirement on a spreadsheet and you have just started what we referred to earlier as a retirement matrix.

When you have completed this step with multiple clients, you can eventually predict what your practice will receive in commissions as much as two years into the future. One building block after another is helping you to establish your base of business, and it will reach a point where it actually builds itself.

Building a team, preparing for growth

The blocks won't keep stacking themselves indefinitely, however, so you need to add a "stacker" to your team. You might find another agent that can do this work, or you may want to hire an administrator. One thing is certain – to grow your business, you need to find such a person. The parrot will stop talking if they find that you didn't properly service some of his or her friends. If you are able to manage your newfound fame by adding staff, you will continue this accelerated growth rate.

It's important not to wait until you have the sad experience of disappointing someone to add staff members to your firm. You have to anticipate the growth and hire beforehand. A line from the movie, "Field of Dreams," states, "if you build it, they will come." The opposite won't work. You can't say, "When they come, I will build it." You must make the investment of office staff first so that you can sustain growth. If you wait, you won't be able to manage the growth as it comes – and come it will.

You have to envision yourself reaching the goal before it happens. Someone has said, "IF YOU CAN'T SEE IT, YOU CAN'T BE IT." This might sound like an odd expression, but to borrow from the world of surfing, once you begin to build your pipeline you have to anticipate what's going to happen so you can stay ahead of the curl of the wave. You have to start finding more companies to work with. By adding staff, you can ensure that your existing business will be handled properly while you are searching the horizon for more.

Another thing I like to do is keep on hand a list of all the clients I work with at a particular company. That way, new clients can see how many of their co-workers already use my firm. And if you are fortunate enough to have a client provide you with a company directory, you will have a ready-made call list complete with the ages of employees, cell telephone numbers, etc. Each of these treasures is a building block – and you will be amazed at how easy they are to obtain.

A little 'Thank You' goes a long way

It's very important for me to let my clients know how much I appreciate getting referrals from them. It might involve a phone call to thank them, or a handshake with me telling them, "Thank you," in person. Sometimes I hand out a small gift, such as a coffee mug, fountain pen, or a shirt with my firm's logo. There are many products we purchase strictly for "giveaways" to show our appreciation.

Sometimes I will take a client out for lunch as a thank you. They appreciate gestures like that, and it increases your business. We will discuss total referral systems in the next chapter, but for now we are just dealing with fundamentals.

The same concept works with your staff. If there is no incentive for them to profit from the growth of your retirement business other than keeping their job, then that's the same kind of effort you can expect: They will work just enough to keep their job. You need to structure your organization in such a way that as your business grows, the staff is just as excited about the growth as you are. You can provide things like bonus levels, vacation days, or a two-night stay at a nice hotel.

The goal is quite simple. If you grow, they grow. And the opposite must also be true: If you go backwards, so do they. You want to be a team, and teams have leaders, not bosses. This idea of prospering together and not prospering together isn't a threat. It's a challenge, and a very exciting one because it allows them to participate directly in what you experience. What is this feeling we are experiencing? It is the knowledge that our business is taking off. Notice that I intentionally said, "our" business – because that's what it will be, not just "mine" or "yours."

Searching for golden headlines

In some cases, as we noted earlier, an ideal opportunity may present itself when we pick up the newspaper and notice that XYZ Company is going to have to release 2,000 employees in the next five months. This kind of report might be disconcerting for the employees involved, but for you, Mr. or Ms. Retirement Planner, this is like gold.

What if someone you had confidence in guaranteed you that there was a vein of gold in the ground and at the same time disclosed to you the general area of ground where it could be found? They wouldn't need to give you anything more; you'd find a way to get to it, wouldn't you?

You want to look for the companies that are big enough to feed your newly found appetite. The bigger the company, the more prospects for you to recruit. Learn everything you can about the company's retirement plan. Having inside knowledge is like adding gasoline to a fire. It's going to be hard to slow the process down, and impossible to put the fire out.

Your understanding of the company's retirement plan can be improved even more if you can become familiar with the company's retirement services managers. I'm referring to the individuals that will actually be processing the paperwork for a retiree to leave. You simply need to put your team in a position to know who to call to get the prospective retiree's paperwork processed. This will put you in a position to rapidly repeat the function because of your newly formed relationship with the team that performs this task.

Identifying the 'professors'

The process of achieving a stronghold in a company requires the help of two kinds of employees. The first is the friendly "parrot," the person we have talked about previously. The second type is the kind I like to call "the professor." The professor may be just as well known as the parrot, but for different reasons. These individuals review a situation in microscopic detail before making a decision. The other employees are aware of this trait and realize the professor must have tried hard to find flaws in your plan. The new prospect feels comfortable in the knowledge that if there were a problem with your proposal, the professor would have found it. In many cases, they will have told you just that.

I think it is safe to say that it is just as important to have *professors* that have placed their business with you, as it is to have *parrots* that have done the same thing. Both will help you increase your retirement business because, in their own way, each feels that they are part of it. You definitely want to include the professors on the list of names you show a new prospect, since they may not know these individuals have already placed their trust in you.

The professors are usually not like the parrot, at least in terms of spreading the good news. They will not tell the other employees about you, so you have to tell your new prospect about them.

Where to do what you do

The dynamics of seeing your retirement business transition from that first prospecting call and grow into a multi-million dollar practice is just a matter of how well the news gets delivered. We have talked so far about word-of-mouth delivery, specifically via the parrots and the professors. We have reviewed the staffing required and the systems it takes to keep the ball rolling and the pipeline full. This is now the time to take a giant growth step and talk about *where* to do this work.

That would be in your office, not at the client's office, not at their kitchen table, and not at your favorite restaurant. Those places just simply won't do. It has to be at *YOUR OFFICE.* That's what gives you "home field advantage," and if you don't have a home field, then you need to get one.

That's where the magic happens; that's where you turn their dream into reality; that's where you have all the power; and that's what they want to see. This is a crucial decision. I am not saying that the whole process hinges on this point, but to compromise this vital part of the process can seriously impact your results. Here are some reasons:

You can literally see 25 to 30 clients in a 44-hour workweek if it is done in *your office*. You can't see half that many if you are driving around the countryside. You can accomplish during one meeting in *your office* the same amount of work that takes two or three meetings on the road. Tell your prospect these things – tell them it's going to be better for them to come to you than for you to go to them. You can and must make them understand.

A lot of prospects come in because they have been offered an early-out package and the decision has to be made by the employee quickly. He has to decide "fast," and if he or she is not quick enough, the package will be offered to someone else. In most cases, there is no time for several "in-home" meetings to discuss this crucial decision. The only place where you have enough back up to support your advice is in your office. Your staff is located there, and they will be able to run the documentation necessary to help your prospect make a decision quickly. And in most cases, your prospect will be able to review all aspects of this all-important decision in a single meeting.

The family doctor didn't quit making house calls just because he was lazy. It was really a decision that saved lives. If he got to their house without the right equipment or medicine, they died. The crucial medicine or equipment he needed was located in his office. The doctor of old didn't want to continue to lose patients, so he changed his practice. Likewise, we don't want to lose any of our "patients."

Using 'home court' to your advantage

I am not saying it's easy to convince them at first, but once you establish this fact, it's the turning point – you won't have to cover this ground again. We spent most of this chapter establishing the point that *good news travels fast*. What you have to do now is make sure the prospects understand that the good news is transmitted at *your office*.

It's much better for them because all of your base material is there. It's better for them, and without question it's better for you. This is the point at which things begin to travel at light speed. You can start to work with another agent, and the two of you and your staff can handle the business as fast as it comes at you.

The update meeting and the contract delivery meeting both take place at *your office.* This is the fastest way to spread the good news. This is where the clients come to get their mugs, pens, gift certificates, golf shirts, and any other free items that you think will enhance the business. This is the place they bring their friends to "meet the wizard." This is the "OZ" of the retirement planning business.

This is also where the prospect received the heart that allowed them to walk out of the workplace and go home to the spouse they love. It's the place where the prospect received the courage to tell his boss without blinking that forty years is enough. This is the place where the prospect received the knowledge that allowed them to start living their dreams of retirement because now they have been able to look thirty years into the future and know it will be all right.

This is the place where the client found shelter from the Wicked Witch. She wasn't allowed to eat up their retirement income with evil taxes. They weren't persuaded by the Witch to choose the wrong retirement option. They didn't fall in the pit of despair where they found out their income was forever lost because of a stock market decline. They were delivered from all of these, as well as many other retirement-threatening calamities, by the Wizard. This "Wizard" – who by now you should realize – resides in your office.

They received the good news at your office. The yellow brick road didn't come to them; on the contrary, they followed it to OZ. They followed it to you, and folks, the success of your business, your ability to dig up that gold just waiting for you in your back-yard, all still turns on this one point:

GOOD NEWS REALLY DOES TRAVEL FAST.

Chapter Four:

THE IMPORTANCE OF GETTING REFERRALS

"There's gold in them thar hills!"

You've heard the saying, "There's gold in them thar hills!"? Popular opinion has it that these words were first spoken in Dahlonega, Georgia, scene of one of the lesser-known gold rush towns in the United States. These words were expressed to encourage the prospectors not to leave the area in search of much greater returns in California. Of course, we know about California and that many struck it rich there. But we don't have to do a lot of research to know many that risked so much ended up losing everything in the process.

At this point I'm sure I don't have to impress upon the reader of this book the importance of referrals, or that gaining them (or not gaining them) can make or break any sales business. This chapter will assume that you already accept this well-known fact. What might not be well known is the process of how to obtain this shiny "ore" that makes your business glow.

The voice of reason that was declared in Dahlonega will be echoed in this chapter. We will not be attempting to show you how to use radio, television, or expensive seminars to get referrals. What we are attempting to provide you in this chapter is a means for getting the referral that doesn't put your business at risk in the process of finding these most precious gems. There was gold in California, but getting to it took great risk and cost lives. We want to listen to the voice of the mayor of Dahlonega and gather the gold that is within our grasp, but avoid the job-threatening risks.

For instance, the individual that you bought the expensive dinner for to gain a professional introduction would probably have given you the same referral for a three-dollar fountain pen. What's even more amazing is that many of these individuals will give you the information just because he or she wishes to help you – with no expectation of receiving anything in return.

Referrals: Never let a day go to waste

The most important part of this process is that you have to be working on it each and every day. The gold mine doesn't produce if you don't. This isn't something that happens on special occasions, or when you have saved up for a radio spot. This is our lifeblood, and it better be pumping each and every day.

Even the first time we meet with a prospect, we should be wondering who they might know that needs this same service. Returning to our gold rush analogy for a moment, the only thing that was in the prospector's mind when he discovered a large nugget in a north Georgia River was a simple question: *How many more like this are in that water?*

The most important goal you and I should have is to get as many referrals in a week as we possibly can. We want at least five, but we would like even more. ***Please write this goal and check your results every week.*** No exceptions.

The reason this goal is emphasized above is based on one simple fact: It's nearly impossible to fail in this business if you meet this goal.

- *When you are performing your annual update on an existing client, ASK FOR REFERRALS.*
- *When you are delivering a contract to a new client, ASK FOR REFERRALS.*
- *When you are having your annual Christmas parties, ASK FOR REFERRALS.*

- *When you are meeting a prospect for the first time, even in that environment, ASK FOR REFERRALS.*

If you don't ask for referrals, I assure you that you certainly won't receive any. The opposite is also true. If you ask, in most cases you will receive. You won't have to go to California to get the gold. It is right here, all around you!

I was told when I first started work for my current employer to ask for three referrals a week – *and that you were to do this only when you knew clients well enough or long enough.*

This directive was far too scientific for me. How would I know when was it time for me to ask? And why was I asking for *three* – and no more or less?

Here are some likely results if I ask someone for three referrals: The referral source can only think of two, but since they were asked for three, they won't give you any. Can you see the problem with that?

This one is even better: They know ten people they could refer, but because you only asked for three, they will give you *only three.* The hard-working, determined miner in Georgia was simply looking for nuggets, and he would take any kind of map he could get his hands on that could help him. Similarly, the number of referrals you ask for is not important; how long you know the person is not important; and how you ask for the referral is not important. WHAT *IS* IMPORTANT IS THAT YOU ASK!

It's the results that matter

Start planning for the gold and make sure that anyone who helps you in your quest gets some type of reward from you. These are gold nuggets, folks, and you just want to mine them. You don't care about the process. *It's the results that matter.*

Is it really that important? We need a quick review by way of comparison: Statistically we are taught that ten calls made to potential clients will get you three appointments, and three appointments will get your one sale. Those same ten calls placed to individuals referred to you, however, will get you *eight* appointments, and the eight appointments will get you *four* sales. That's a four-hundred percent improvement! I like those statistics much better, don't you?

The credit card companies have special cards for their most prized clients, and they call them platinum cards. We have that same standard for our client base – we call them "platinum clients." These individuals know they're platinum and they know why. They know it's *not* because they have more money invested with our firm than any other clients. It's because of the help they give us!

We have special dinners for our platinum clients, and we honor them and their impact on our business at those dinners. These are the clients who send us the most referrals. They aren't the only ones giving us referrals, nor are they the only clients we are rewarding. It's just that they have just reached the top echelon of our referral charts. At the same time, they have pushed us to the top.

You would probably want to become a platinum firm, and to accomplish that goal you need to have platinum clients – so you can mine the gold! The following paragraphs list different ways to gain – and retain – these most important of all clients.

Ways to go prospecting

Annual Christmas Party: This event is one of the best places to incorporate this process, and you are probably already hosting this event. Here you simply make the biggest door prize the property of the person who supplies you with the largest list of referrals. We actually have a sign-in sheet at our Christmas party where people can list referrals for us to contact. The form we provide has a place for the referral's name, phone number, and age.

Some of our more competitive clients will work on their list the entire party, while others will choose not to participate in this contest. We had one individual who kept working on his list at our party just trying to win a seventy-five dollar mall gift certificate for his daughter. He eventually won the certificate, but he gave us so many referrals that my firm was the big winner. This will work for you because people love contests.

At our party the next year, the contest was settled almost before it started. One of our clients came with his list already prepared. He was determined to win the prize that year and his list had names, cell phone numbers, ages, and approximate retirement dates for every individual at the company where he worked.

The referral list this individual provided proved to be worth about $70,000 in revenues over the next four or five months. In fact, we are *still* using that particular list today, three years later. Yes, we are still mining it for nuggets.

Without question, this was money well-spent by my firm on a gift certificate! *This was the GOLD we were hoping to find.*

Annual client reviews are another fertile area in hunting for this all-important mineral for building your business. We make it a part of every update to ask if the person being reviewed knows anyone that we can help. We give out mugs, fountain pens, or Cracker Barrel gift certificates for the bounty we collect at those meetings. These are very inexpensive gifts, but the gesture is important to the client because it shows our appreciation.

The Annual Review: I want to digress just a bit from referrals at this point. There are some financial professionals that might feel an annual review is a waste of time. I personally disagree. This is a great opportunity to learn more about your client. You aren't pressured to make a sale, and they are under no pressure because they're already your clients. This is a time when your bond with them can be strengthened.

You can update yourself on their family situation, along with updating their portfolio. This is the meeting where you can become aware of any changes in their life that might warrant attention from you. Maybe they have a need to increase life insurance, or perhaps they have some additional money available to invest. This meeting can be where you learn about their aging parents and begin to explore ways for eliminating their worries about the long-term care issue. And this can become the meeting where you help them establish a trust that can be used to take care of an adult child that will never be able to take care of himself or herself.

This is the door you use to enter the private corners of their lives without any feelings of intrusion. There is no area more important to strengthening your business than this meeting – their annual review. In my firm, holding these meetings accounts for 40% of all new business.

So let me state it simply: If you aren't already doing these reviews, *YOU NEED TO START.*

Retirement parties: Retirement parties are commonly thrown for the new retiree by their former employer. It is not so common, however, for someone like a financial professional to throw them a retirement party. But why not do this – and invite a few of their friends who aren't retired yet? Of course, you will also invite their spouse, and they will also want some of their close friends to attend. Can you think of an easier way of going fishing without even having to bait the hook? You didn't seek out referrals. These individuals gave them to you when they created their guest list. The dynamics of the event created this built-in referral base.

An evening like this would also include a lively conversation about who else is nearing or considering retirement, helping to establish your expertise in this area for anyone that is interested.

Putting the money where your referrals are

Everything we have talked about so far is cheaper than ads in the Yellow Pages or in the classifieds, and it directs your advertising budget to the very people that have helped put you where you are. If the editor of your newspaper is one of your most valued clients, I apologize for suggesting you take money out his budget, but I think you see my point.

I don't buy from him because he doesn't buy from me, nor does he or she have contact with the people I am looking for. You couldn't run an ad and get the gold; you had to have someone that could help you find it – and someone able to help you dig it up.

The other item that is essential, and also *just plain right to do,* is being available to help people when they are in need. I am not talking about investment help. A client who becomes very ill should get a card, call or personal visit; whichever of those suits your style. The death of a client in most cases should mean you attend the visitation, the funeral, or both.

An event like this should put your organization into high gear. This is the time where you are the one professional who is helping, but not charging for your services. You are now beginning a process that will prove whether or not you are the person you claim to be. Your organization should process the death claims, regardless of whether there is a dime's worth of money received for this service.

You should help them get Social Security payments started if needed, and assist them in setting up a budget. Many widows and widowers have never paid the bills, and you can help them. Helping people in need might mean simply being a general hand-holder. For them, you have to be the kind of person that you would want to take care of your own mother or father.

This is a test, and it's one **you must pass.** I said earlier that you should do this with no thought of being repaid. But in reality, you definitely will be repaid – in one way or another. You will feel a sense of satisfaction that is almost unbelievable. You will feel better about yourself and know the difference you have made. You might not have delivered a death claim check yet, but if you start working in the area of retirement planning, without question, *you will.* The first time you deliver one of these, your life will never be the same.

Random acts of kindness

You might be wondering why this information is included in the referral section of this book. Therein lies the secret. You will never do anything on purpose that gets you as many referrals as this one random act of kindness you perform. This is the mother load of the referral business – the bonanza of retirement planning.

Helping others always reaps a great return. Your clients will forever be grateful for the assistance you provided during their time of need; they will know you didn't have to do what you did. For you it was simply a part of your job, but many financial professionals just don't do it. They hurt their clients as well as themselves by missing a golden opportunity to make a difference.

You will become familiar with having to file for benefits and death claims from life insurance and pension. You will find yourself becoming established as the "go to" person in this area because, as with many of the other concepts we have discussed, very few offices specialize in this area. True retirement specialists are not engaged in the accumulation of assets; they are involved in the *distribution* of assets. This can and will include the death of a client.

The concept of constantly being vigilant for opportunities to gather referrals continues not just in your annual reviews but also in things like a widow's tea party or luncheon. Activities like this will create a referral source that never dries up, and at the same time it will be so fulfilling that you will not even notice you are cultivating them.

You might find that a newly widowed prospect is brought to your office because of your expertise in this area. You also will discover you have new clients that decided on your firm not because of your vast knowledge, but because of what you did for Jane Doe when her husband died. I can't stress enough that you are not doing this to be repaid from a referral standpoint – you're doing it because it's the right thing to do. Nevertheless, *you will be repaid.*

Golf tournaments and charity events. My organization sometimes sponsors golf tournaments and charity walks, and we give away some nice prizes. However, participants don't buy a raffle ticket to get in the running for one of our prizes. They simply complete an entry form that gives us their name, telephone number, and age, and then they list what kind of financial planning they are interested in learning more about. (On our form we include a checklist of financial services offered).

This puts each one in the drawing for the prizes. Should they decide they want to give themselves more chances to win, and if they will schedule a fact-finder meeting on the spot, extra tickets are given out. On our form we also conveniently provide a place for them to list friends who might be interested in our services. You guessed it: They get extra chances to win prizes for filling out this section of the form! We are looking for gaining referrals in everything we do – because it is yet another way to reach the gold.

No limit to the possibilities

The referral finding business is not a simple one, but because we find it so rewarding, it's exciting to perform. We will do almost anything to try to gain the referrals. If we have a particular client who has never given us any referrals (some people just won't), we like to remind them that the future of our business almost certainly depends on getting referrals. Hopefully they will want to help us stay in business! If we can't get new referrals, the gold vein dries up. Then the business dies, leaving a ghost town where a thriving gold town once stood.

We have sent cookie bouquets or flowers to a retiree's place of employment just before their last day, which always impresses the other employees who also may be thinking of retiring soon. This is like dropping a grenade into an enemy's camp. The difference is, in this case you're not looking for casualties – you're looking for an explosion filled with new referrals. The only "casualty" in this case is your competition. You will get the maximum results when you have several potential retirees in one place.

The most important part of this process is to determine which of these concepts work best for you, and then repeat them over and over again. Hunting for referrals is something that never goes out of style. You never reach a point in your career where this is no longer needed. With practice and repetition, it will become a part of your daily function. Best of all, *it never fails to yield results.* It's like the pan the miner uses to sift for gold: He can't operate without it. And in your work as a retirement planner, you can't continue to operate without referrals.

At this point, it's important to draw a distinction between the analogy we've been using in this chapter – mining for gold – and mining for referrals. There is a distinct difference between the two when we start talking about expected results. The prospector pans the river with a "hope-so" mindset – he's hoping he will find gold. That's not the case, however, when it comes to referrals. The only way you won't strike a rich vein of gold is if you aren't continuing to get the referrals. If you use the referral system to find and continue to cultivate prospects, **you *will* strike gold**. It's not a question of *if;* it's a matter of *how much.*

Keep a list handy of the clients you have from each company you are working with. That way, when you meet with a new prospect from XYZ Company, you will be able to readily identify people there who are already working with your firm. This is a good business practice and gives you added credibility with the prospect, knowing that so many of his co-workers trust you.

These ideas are not unique. But the possibility that they won't work and you won't strike it rich by using those you like best is non-existent. The vein of gold is endless, and there is enough to be mined to last for your entire career.

The miner never found himself in a situation where the gold would come to him, no matter how good his instincts were. You, however, know a secret that can create a flow of gold that comes to you. You will find that if you work the referral system long and hard enough, the prospects will call you! That's right: No coaxing, no pushing, no begging; they just call you and ask for a meeting.

You will find there are times when you didn't see it coming, that you didn't even have them on your list of potential clients, and they called you. You didn't mine it; it just appeared. The more you work the referral system, and the better you become at it, the more times this exciting phenomenon will occur.

The area of the country doesn't matter, as it did in the days of the gold rush. Georgia and California are equal in opportunity – and so is any other state you might name. You could spend thousands of dollars in advertising and end up going out of business just like the miners of old; or you can listen to the voice of reason.

As I assured you at the start of this chapter,

THERE *IS* GOLD IN THEM THAR HILLS.

You just needed to know how to find it – and now you do!

Chapter Five:

MANAGEMENT AND SYSTEMS FOR STAYING ON TOP

In other words, "Let's get this process on autopilot!"

Now we are getting to the "boring stuff," at least compared to what we've been discussing – but it's also the kind of information that will keep your business running smoothly. Besides, once your business takes off, you will be having so much fun, you won't even remember the meaning of the word *boring*.

A pilot will probably tell you that it is much more exciting to fly the plane themselves than to place it on autopilot. But sometimes they need the plane to fly itself. Automobiles offer a similar feature. Sometimes it's helpful to place the car on cruise control. We have those systems in place in a plane and a vehicle for good reason. You can get by without them, but why would you want to? I don't think anyone gets excited about how a clock works, but it sure is hard to get somewhere on time if the one you're using is not working.

Let me tell you about a few of the "autopilot" methods we use in our firm. Remember in a previous chapter when we talked about the importance of annual reviews? Remember how exciting they were? Well, you won't get that excitement if you don't have a system in place to trigger the event.

The two-card system

In our company we employ a two-card system and it works well for us. But this, as well as most of the rest of this chapter, can be changed or adapted to fit your own firm. The key point to remember is that you do need to have a system in place because the autopilot is necessary.

Now that we have that out of the way, back to the two-card system: When the prospect becomes a client, we establish two cards. The first card tells their birthday and the other one is the date they first entered into a contract. The cards are placed in a file by order of the date. This means that every client is going to have at least two touches every year from my office. They will receive a birthday card at the appropriate time, and they also will receive a letter on their anniversary date that indicates it is time to come in and have their annual review performed.

The update meeting, as we previously stated, is not just to update their portfolio. The meeting is also intended to do new business that the client has previously expressed interest in, and to acquire those all-important referrals. The update meeting letter doesn't indicate that they should *think* about coming by, it indicates *it is time* for them to come in. The letter or card you receive from your dentist sends doesn't indicate that you *might* want to come in. It directly states that it is time to come in.

This is your clients' financial future and it is every bit as important as getting their teeth cleaned regularly. So you don't want to hope that the autopilot works. You want to build it in such a way that you know for certain that it does work.

Following up on the Fact Finder meeting

Another area where we felt the need for creating an autopilot system involved the follow-up to an initial meeting. We call the initial meeting a "Fact Finder meeting." The fact finder we use concludes with a final question that says, "Are You Interested In Further Discussions?" Obviously, when someone answers that question in the affirmative, we are called into action. To make sure nothing falls through the cracks, we rely on our autopilot system.

Within a few days, we send a form letter that refers them back to the answer they gave to that all-important question. The letter mentions we were pleased that they indicated an interest in proceeding with further discussions and meetings concerning the next step for their retirement future. The letter also tells them they will be getting a call from us to schedule that meeting.

You see, we are not asking them if they are interested, because they have already said they are. We are simply following up on their request for further discussions to take place.

We're grooming them for this kind of service, just as your dentist does. The dentist doesn't send a letter that asks if you want to take care of your teeth. You told the dentist you wanted to take care of your teeth when you hired him or her. We also have similar letters to address various concerns the client has, such as life insurance, long-term care, and other needs.

We never assume clients have changed their mind unless they inform us that they have. We want the whole process to be on autopilot with the client, just as the pilot does. If our clients want to turn it off, they know how.

Keeping track of key dates

There are certain dates other than the client's birthday that we regard as very important. We have an age matrix that indicates when a client reaches one of these critical times. The age 60 is one such date. The reason this age is important is quite simple: Their 401(k) will, in most cases, allow the removal of all their funds through an in-service withdrawal. This is not something the client always remembers or understands, and it is very important for you or your staff to remind them.

Just to touch once again on the in-service withdrawal, this is the company plan allowing an employee to withdraw a percentage of their funds while still employed. That percentage at age sixty is one hundred percent. This is not a date you want to trust to your memory, because if you forget it too many times, you might find that your competition has stepped in and is moving your client's money. I think if you didn't see it before, you can certainly see now why the systems are important.

We need the same kind of matrix to make sure we know when the client is retiring. They will give you that date when you are doing their retirement module. Once again, you don't want to rely on your memory to keep up with it. Hence the advantage of "autopilot."

As I have stated previously, it is very important to make sure you have a list from each company you are prospecting that tells you the names of all of your clients from that particular company. This will allow you to have a conversation with a new prospect from any of these companies, recite the names of the clients you have already acquired, and do it at the speed of light. You want to make them feel that all of their friends are with you already and that they are being left out. You can't accomplish that task if you're doing it by memory.

Building a matrix to track status

You also need a life insurance matrix that shows which clients you have done presentations for and the current status of that work. A rollover status is also important: You must be able to keep up with the signed rollover forms so that the money gets invested in the new accounts quickly.

This next point is very important. ***Don't let the company that will be the new trustee for the money process the rollover. You and I should do it – we want the money in the account more than they do.*** So we need to control our own destiny.

You probably don't need any help in this next area, so we will make it brief. You need to have a folder of information on retirement for your initial meeting, material they will get to take home. I know about compliance, but please give them more than a prospectus about the products. They are buying your firm, not the company that produces the products, so you want them to carry a little of you home with them. Anything less is just plain boring, and bored is the last thing you want them to feel when they leave your office!

You should give them plenty of information on retirement planning. They need to see that you are well qualified and prepared to help them with this important issue. If you are not equipped to handle this issue, then get yourself a partner and let this person supply this critical information. You might think that you don't know anyone to partner with, but if you set many of these meetings, you won't have any trouble finding someone willing to help you with it. We all know that getting the meeting scheduled is the hardest part.

I think it goes without saying, but we're going to say it anyway and we'll probably say it more than once: You aren't the person who is setting up the two-card system, mailing out follow-up or initial letters, or putting together a packet of information for the prospect. *You will want to outsource these tasks as quickly as your practice will allow!* You are the *idea* person. You're the person who sets the meetings and closes the sale.

Think of it this way: The pilot doesn't try to fly the plane when it's on autopilot, and you don't have to depress the gas pedal when the car is on cruise control. This needs to become a well-oiled machine, and it only stays that way if you do your part – and leave the other parts alone. You start your business as the person who does all of these things, but you need to get out of the way as soon as possible.

The quarterback doesn't play all positions

This business is going to end up with a lot of the retired clients getting monthly checks. You will need help in making sure this part of your business is working correctly. There is nothing that will lose the business you worked so hard to obtain quicker than someone not getting their check. That's one reason you can't allow yourself to get caught up in the machinery. You are the quarterback, which means you must understand each position and its role, but you are only to play your position.

The opposite is also true. The staff can operate the systems for you, but they don't create them. That's your job. You will need a system as mentioned earlier to make sure the client gets their monthly check. This will also entail making sure the money for that check comes from a fixed fund. You don't want their need for a monthly check dictating when the stocks are sold. That must be determined by you.

You also want to make sure the clients understand that they don't want to take money out of an IRA and pay taxes on it only to put it in the bank, draw interest, and pay taxes on it again. These processes are controlled by your staff and once again, remember that they have to be operating on *autopilot.*

Key ingredient: a skilled manager

The makeup of your staff should include one person who is a skilled manager. This is the hardest piece of the machinery to procure – because this person needs to share your understanding of how to do financial planning. This person isn't easy to find, because if they have the licensing requirements to perform your task, why would they want to work for you when they could do the same thing on their own?

This is the one part of setting up this entire process that's somewhat hard to accomplish, but if you can find this person, it becomes a marriage made in heaven. Your team will be unbeatable. This individual needs to have a different skill set than you do. You can sell concepts, and either they can't or do not wish to do so. They love to perform the tasks that go along with retirement planning, but they desire to do it from the backroom. You, however, can accomplish backroom tasks but would rather be in front of the client.

Once you can identify this person and bring them onto your team, you both find yourselves performing within your areas of strength and a winning combination is born. This type of partner-ship requires almost no training on your part and very little start-up time.

I'm not saying that it is essential to have a former agent run-ning your staff – or being your entire staff support – but if you can establish such a relationship, then the machine definitely runs much more efficiently. The most important thing is that you find someone capable of doing this behind-the-scenes work. *You do not need to be performing this kind of task.*

Software can easily paint the picture

In addition, you obviously need some kind of software to illustrate a retirement plan so the prospective client can see on paper what type of spending pattern they can afford without running out of money before death. The plan should be designed to show the difference between the company option for spousal protection, as we discussed previously, and pension maximization using life insurance. These reports should allow the client to analyze when he or she will retire, and that allows you to position them on the Retirement Matrix.

You need to have a report that is adaptable to the client's needs. For example, if a client is offered an early out, this will allow you to show them how the offer changes the plan you had previously established. This part of the planning process is very important, and the speed at which you perform the task is equally important, because in many cases they don't have a lot of time to review the offer. A delay on your part might mean the offer is given to another employee that was able to make the decision more quickly. The potential client might even find another finan-cial professional who can do this quickly and as a result, your sale is lost.

Retirement modules are good, but since speed is of the essence, you can simply create a plan showing the gap between working and retiring. This can be done very simply on a whiteboard.

Remember: *You must have the staff so you can provide these answers quickly.*

You need to have some sort of update form that indicates when you last met with your client and summarizes the information gathered from that meeting. You obviously need to know the recommendations you offered at that meeting and whether or not they were followed. But don't count on your memory to supply that information – especially if your client list continues to expand, as I'm certain it will.

Your physician, for example, has to make sure you took the prescription he gave you. It doesn't matter how long you have been a patient. How can the doctor do this if they don't have a record indicating what the prescription was? This form you prepare should also indicate a buildup of assets, which allows you to know when to make recommendations on estate planning.

Remember, you are the Retirement Doctor, and this is your "medical log." *You must maintain all the information pertaining to your financial "patient."* And I can't emphasize this enough: Make sure you have a place on that update form for them to write in some referrals!

The proof is in the facilities

You will also need certain facilities at your disposal. We have previously indicated that it is very important to have the home-field advantage. That being said, it probably goes without saying that you need an actual "home-field." This amounts to an office and if possible, access to several conference rooms.

In our office, we offer a variety of drinks and snacks when someone arrives, and we also have an ample supply of magazines about retirement for them to peruse before we meet with them! There's nothing like whetting their appetite before the meeting. Our clients also like chocolate (who doesn't?) so we always have bowls of M&M's and other wrapped candies available in our conference rooms. When they don't avail themselves of this option, we do. (I didn't say we were in good physical shape!)

This chapter is about trying to get you in good financial shape. There can always be a reaction to each activity you do for your clients; in many instances it is not foreseen, but the results can be incredibly positive. We started the M&M's idea two years ago, even though we had no relationship with the producer of that product. Today, we have 30 or so clients that worked for the M&M/Mars Company! So our little candy offering definitely sweetened the pot, so to speak. And now, back to the main subject – your facilities.

Your client files should obviously be in the immediate vicinity for you and your staff. In my office, we have a centrally located file room. My staff sets up a conference room for an upcoming appointment. They also greet our prospects or clients as they arrive, offer them refreshments, and seat them in the reception area until it's time for their meeting. My staff is wonderful at conversing with everyone who walks through the door. They make everyone feel welcome and special.

Before I enter the conference room to conduct the meeting, my staff has briefed me on any personal updates, just as a nurse would brief a physician before they enter the exam room. There should be several fact-finder packets already made up and available in case you have the good fortune of having someone drop in unscheduled.

The conference room should be equipped with reallocation forms, distribution forms, tax bracket charts, etc. This will allow you to stay in front of your client instead of leaving the room in search of whatever document you might require. Make sure you anticipate any eventualities so that you're prepared. You don't want to react; you want to be on *autopilot*.

You probably will have compliance reviews, audits, or whatever name fits this exciting situation. This is another case where your skilled staff can prepare you for this annual event so you can continue concentrating on and taking care of your clients. You have to take the lead and create the system to be ready for the event, but the staff must perform all the preparatory activities.

In readiness for the referrals

Your team will prepare for the "Top Referral Dinner" previously mentioned in the referral section. The whole process runs as a team with each person doing their part, like a smooth-running car engine with all pistons firing in concert. They can help select the guests for this event, mail out the invitations, and get party favors and activities planned out.

Then comes the fun part: We spend the whole afternoon making the platinum clients feel extra special – because *they are*! We lavish a lot of praise on them as though they were the most important persons we know. I'm sure you noticed my use of the word *we*. I can't do this alone very well. It takes a team to make the evening special. That's essentially what an autopilot, TV remote control, and cruise control are all about. It's one unit doing a lot of things at one time. And that's what happens at this dinner – several people are acting together as one unit. It's a seamless product and, with a little practice, it works like cruise control.

The systems that the team implements will find the referrals, tell us when the existing client is going to retire, and make sure we know whenever someone has just experienced a windfall, such as inheriting a lot of money or winning the lottery.

I know it sounds ridiculous to think that a system will do all these things and more. But we live in a society where computers do a lot of the work that agents previously performed. Doesn't it then make sense that we can develop systems to remember things for us and create new business for our firm? Computers don't think, but your staff members do. You simply have to understand the blueprint, and once you do, you can build a reliable mechanism for performing the work. Imitating the industrial revolutionaries, you can build the systems that allow you to work less and accomplish much more.

We have probably not covered every system it takes to accomplish the work we have discussed in previous chapters. But I think we have addressed enough of the issues that the message is clear. We also didn't spell out how many staff members you will need or the exact dimensions of your office. These and many other items are a matter of choice.

That's the exciting thing about this kind of work. You get to choose how you want your business to be set up. You are in charge of your own destiny. This brings us back to the original idea we presented at the beginning of this chapter: It is up to the pilot to decide if he wants to use the autopilot or not. And it's up to the driver to decide if he wants to use the cruise control or not. In the same way, it's up to you whether you put any of this into place or not.

You can walk over and turn on the television, and then get up again each time you need to change the channel – or you can pick up the remote control and use it. In this case, at least from a male's standpoint, we know they are definitely going with the remote. The point is you can choose to do all of the items in this chapter by yourself and work all the extra hours to accomplish the task on your own, if you prefer. But just like the pilot who sometimes uses the autopilot; the driver who sometimes uses the cruise control; or the guy who picks up the television remote control, sometimes it's nice not to have to do all the work!

JUST PUT YOUR SYSTEMS ON AUTOPILOT AND MOVE TO THE NEXT LEVEL.

You'll be glad you did.

Chapter Six:

WHAT TYPES OF PRODUCTS SHOULD BE USED?

Wake up and smell the coffee!

Generally, when someone directs the phrase "Wake up and smell the coffee" toward someone else, the target of this admonition doesn't find it an endearing statement. While the interpretation can vary, the general thought behind this phrase is *pay attention to what's happening in your environment.* Your wedding day, for instance, is not the time that you should start kicking around the pros and cons of committing to marriage. Nor is it the time to be making a decision about which person you should be marrying.

Major decisions like these fit another time and place, and should have already been settled by that point in the process. But if not, *wake up and smell the coffee!* So for the context of our discussion, we are in the business of helping people plan for retirement. For that reason, the *type of product* is not as important as *fitting a particular product to the situation* you are dealing with.

There are many examples of this, but here's one typical scenario of fitting a particular product to the situation: You find yourself with a prospect in your office who has already turned down his company's plan to take care of his wife in the event of his death. The option he chose pays out more per month during his lifetime, but it ends when he dies.

He finds himself in a tough situation if he does not do something at this point. If he dies prematurely, his spouse will have no pension, no husband, and maybe very little in the way of assets. The type of stock you might buy this couple, or whether you purchase an annuity or mutual fund, will have very little effect on their current situation. This person should have consulted someone like you before he made his decision, but he didn't, so you have to work with the circumstances as they are at the moment.

The situation you're dealing with is not the one that brought him to your office. He thought you were going to discuss how to invest his 401(k) assets. This person indicated he wanted his spouse in the meeting with you in order to make sure the investments you are using for their retirement are suitable for both of them. The pension benefit he took is only suitable for someone that is not married, or doesn't care what happens to their spouse if they die.

Who needs to 'wake up'?

If the subject of life insurance is not raised by the financial professional at this point, then it's the advisor that needs to *wake up and smell the coffee.* If the subject of life insurance does come up and the prospective client doesn't feel good about that conversation, then he is the one that needs to *wake up and smell the coffee.* If he doesn't want to talk about life insurance at this point, then he should have taken an option from the company to protect the pension in the event of his premature death. There isn't anything that's going to take care of a widow's future as well as some type of life insurance benefit can.

The reason I said, "Wake up and smell the coffee," is because he has already turned down the company benefit. As a consequence, we now have to make the prospective widow our highest priority, taking steps to safeguard her financial security.

The type of life insurance isn't a huge issue in this case, but what is important is that the right tool gets used to fix the situation. That tool, most certainly, is life insurance. However, this might be a product that you aren't very proficient at using. If that is the case, as we previously stated, you just need to find someone who has this important expertise and partner with them.

The right solution to each situation is much more important than finding a really good product and trying to match it to every client's situation. You might find that as a retirement doctor, some patients won't take the medicine you prescribe, and in that case you can't save them. This doesn't mean you can't still be their doctor, but it also never relieves you of the responsibility of tying to fix their problem.

Once you find the solution, the product can take many forms. In the case I referred to above, since you were prescribing life insurance, there were several options: You could have prescribed permanent life, term life, or a combination of the two. Your expertise on which life insurance company to use and the exact application is important, and your knowledge is extremely valuable. But the solution is where you earn your money and gain your reputation. There are cases where finding the right solution will gain you nothing in terms of money, but will leave you satisfied that you have done your job and that your reputation has been enhanced dramatically.

When you finish the job – but the job isn't done

I want to give a personal example of this: My office was working with a client on a rollover from a company plan that included a lump sum and a 401(k). We had the right product, which in this case happened to be an annuity with an income and death benefit rider. We completed the complicated company paperwork to make this rollover happen correctly, and that concluded a task that had started two years before. This rollover and the continued management of the funds would supply my team a pretty good influx of capital.

It would seem that we had completed our job, having done the correct thing for our client. As it turned out, we were not finished.

As my business manager poured over the paperwork, he noticed that our client could continue to pay the premium on his company life insurance and would be given guaranteed insurability. The price for continuing the coverage was very expensive and could only be carried for five more years, even after the employee paid $1,000 per month. However, in this case the five years didn't matter, nor did the price, because our client was dying of cancer.

This client lived just long enough to make one payment in the amount of $1,000, and his widow collected *three hundred thousand dollars.* The meeting we had conducted initially was to talk about the right investment for them. We had spent weeks finding just the right one and positioning the portfolio within the annuity correctly. The most important sale that day, however, was the one we didn't create; it was the one that made my company no money, and the one that did the most to maintain the dignity of a dying man.

We had the right product for the client. We were in a meeting to talk only about the idea that we sold. These were the facts, but if we had not taken notice of his situation and the opportunity to take advantage of an important company benefit, we would have missed the real solution to their problem. We would have carried through only on part of what the client trusted us to do.

Remember, we are planning retirement, and *retirement is not a product, it's not a company, it's not a place. It's a process,* a process that enables us to recognize situations like this: the fact that our client was not retiring because he got an early-out opportunity. He was retiring because he was dying. That was the focus on his part, and therefore it needed to be our focus also – and it was.

Though it would seem like we did a pretty good job, based on the death benefit of the annuity, in this case we would still have belonged to the crowd that needs to *wake up and smell the coffee.*

Even the best products are only tools

There is no substitute for finding the right solution to the client's situation. While it's equally important to put the client into the best product on the market, that product is still merely a tool for you to use for working on their situation.

Whenever you find a great product, that's exciting, and much of the excitement is because you know how much help it will be to your client. The problem is, that doesn't separate you from the field of advisors who don't study retirement work but can buy the very same product.

Let's put it this way: When the client came to your office, they were not looking for a saw or a hammer; they wanted to find a carpenter to help them build their dream retirement plan. We must never confuse the individual product for the solution. I trust you are beginning to see this more clearly.

The kind of scalpel is not the most important thing when someone needs open-heart surgery. The important thing, rather, is the surgeon who is holding it and that person's skill and expertise in its use.

When we mentioned how to determine what products to use, it must always be the one that best fits the situation. This might sound like it could be very confusing or difficult to understand, and you certainly don't want to make a mistake when dealing with something this important. But the answer is much simpler than it sounds. You just have to put yourself in their place, and the right product will become apparent.

We might have made our example seem more complicated than it was. If you had put yourself in the shoes of a dying client who is actually planning his wife's retirement, you would have found the life insurance too. You didn't have to research the options. There was only one, and you would have seen it if you were using your expertise to look through his eyes.

Great product for wrong situation – the wrong product!

This is true for every situation. You may have some really good blue chip stocks and a client who is very excited about having you load them into their retirement portfolio. But if this client needs a great deal of income, the vast majority of the portfolio is going to have to be invested in products that will meet the income need. Great product – and great expertise on your part – but this was the wrong situation.

Don't forget that unless a client forces you to do otherwise, if it's the wrong product for the situation, don't use it. You want to have the reputation as the financial professional who met their needs, not the one who has the best products. You **gain their trust** by letting them know how efficient you are, but you **keep their trust** by advising them through each new problem, even if many of these situations won't pay you at the time.

There are many cases where the right product is the one they already have. There are also times that the best product is not the one they have, but because of what it costs to leave the current product, they need to keep it – and you and I need to help them manage it. The very best example of this is an annuity with high surrenders. It might not be the best product of its kind, but we have to work with it until it reaches a point where the cost of the surrenders will not cripple the retirement.

What products to use – and what not to use

The title of this chapter indicated we would be discussing what kinds of products are needed, and for the next few pages we are going to do exactly that. However, regardless of the specific product, the overall answer is already presented in the preceding paragraph: *We will not use a product that will cripple the client's retirement.* We need to let that statement be the trail we follow, so that no matter how sleek or brilliant some products seem, they can't deter us from our goal. The goal quite simply is to make certain that the client who no longer works still has income.

The most important thing you can do is to make sure you purchase a product that produces income. Income-producing items like CDs, fixed annuities, bond portfolios, guaranteed income benefit annuities and many others have to fit prominently into the equation. You don't need to use all of them, but you certainly need some of them.

If you happen to believe that CDs are better referred to as "certificates of depreciation" (and I might agree), then you need to find something better to replace them. That can't be your favorite stock. You may even want to use an immediate annuity to provide a great deal of the income and that will allow the client to put more money in equities.

Never betray your client's trust

You must never make the mistake of failing to consider the income need – and never forget that your client put their trust in you to produce it. They may have built a 401(k) that was only invested in stocks, but that was when they were earning a paycheck. They now find themselves having to live off this money and they've hired you to help them do it. Study the products listed in the first part of this section, find the combination that you think will do the job along with determining a percentage of equities needed, and use them to manage the retirement. If you think that you don't need anything but stocks to produce income, or you don't think income is a big consideration, then *you* need to *wake up and smell the coffee.*

When they entered your office and were looking forward to exiting the workforce, they weren't looking for the stock or mutual fund that would make them the most money. That's a sexy concept and you are able to sell it. However, they were worried primarily about two issues that are very important to them: How much will they make now that they don't work, and how much income does their spouse get when they die?

Those two items are about the same concept – and that concept is income. The second question, while still concerning income, deals with income after death. You must deal with income and death. If your products are dealing with anything else as the primary focus (such as maximum gain), then you will unfortunately have to wake up and smell the coffee. You don't want to face a grieving widow and have to tell her the income is destroyed because you were try-ing to make her the most money.

We also need to have products in place to make sure we can pass the remaining assets to the client's heirs. This is always a major consideration because you and I are dealing with retired or retiring clients. The use of life insurance and long-term care to help with the transfer of assets is imperative. Which company you select to provide the long-term care and life insurance isn't the important factor. The important factor is that you use these products.

No such thing as 'just-in-case' here

We have mentioned this before, but it bears repeating: If you don't work with these kinds of products, then you must find someone to partner with that does. You could meet some opposition at this point from your client, but remember you will succeed only if you do the right thing. You need to make sure that you have prepared for all the possibilities that might happen in retirement.

The client might have their house burn, so they probably need fire insurance, and they probably already have it in place. They need car insurance in case they wreck their car, and they probably already have that in place as well. These are just-in-case type prod-ucts, but there is no such thing as just-in-case-they-die.

All of us are going to die, so provision for that is not an option. It's not "just-in case"! Death runs in their family, as it does in yours. You don't need an actuarial table to know the mortality rate is 100%, no exceptions, so we need to always keep that eventuality in mind.

While we are on the subject, they need a will for the same rea-son. You won't make any commissions on this tool, but you and I both know they need one. They came to you for advice – and *not just advice that will make you money.* You don't want to face the adult children of your now-deceased client that are suddenly wrestling with probate issues.

The death of these clients and the intestate estate (no will) is not your fault – as long as you prescribe one, pointing out the need. You can't make your client take the medicine. However, if you didn't prescribe the will because you were too busy trying to make your client and yourself a lot of money, then you are part of the problem.

Those adult children indirectly counted on you to make an efficient transfer of the things their parents worked a lifetime to achieve. Just in case you don't grasp the problem from an ethical vantage point, let's deal with the financial side of things: These folks are your future clients who will have money to invest. The former ones you had, their parents, will be deceased. Your future – and theirs – is at stake.

I have a client who asked me repeatedly to tell him what he needed to make sure his retirement was secure for him and his wife. I told him he needed quite a bit of life insurance. He wanted to take care of the needs, but was frustrated with the solution. He finally told me that if he had to purchase the amount of "love insurance" (that's what I prefer to call it) that I said he needed, he wasn't sure he could still afford his car insurance. Unfazed by his comment, and still driven by his command to build a strong retirement for the two of them, I replied, "Then don't insure the car."

Planning for certainties, not possibilities

My rationale was based on pure fact. I have never met with a grieving widow who indicated that the loss of their husband was magnified because he didn't have any car insurance when he died. But I have met with many who indicated that they didn't know how they were going to make it financially because of a lack of love insurance – love demonstrated by determination to provide for their financial well-being.

I will also admit with a lot of sadness that some of these widows' husbands were my clients before they died. That makes me the person who failed to meet the insurance need, but it wasn't because I didn't try. So if you are not talking to your client about life insurance, then you need to *wake up and smell the coffee.*

I don't mean to make these solutions sound simple. The reason more people don't have love insurance is because unlike car insurance, it doesn't supply a benefit to the owner; it supplies a benefit for someone they love. I never indicated that this whole process was simple to administer. I merely said that it's simple to understand.

There is also a much higher chance that a retired person will need to go to a long-term care facility than the chance that a fire will occur at their residence. Once again, this means you and I need to understand the different products associated with selling long-term care and life insurance.

You might be starting to think the title for this chapter was misleading. It wasn't. The title was correct. The best product is the one that fits a person's needs for retirement. But the needs of all retirees bear many similarities. So the good news is this: If you find a very good product that fits the important needs of retirees, you will get to use it over and over again.

Common needs of retirees

The following is a list of the common retiree's needs, in no particular order:

1. They need protection against living too long and not having income.
2. They need protection against dying too soon and not providing income for their spouse.
3. They need protection against having their assets depleted to pay for long-term health care.
4. They need protection from the rising cost of health care and Medicare supplements.
5. They need to be confident that their assets will pass to their loved ones in the event of their death, in the most tax-efficient manner.

The products that take care of these issues are weapons you and I will use to defeat any forces that would attempt to negatively affect the client's retirement years. Always remember it is not the product that takes care of the situation; rather it is the financial professional that is using that product.

Again, when and if you were to experience the need for a heart operation, you wouldn't care what kind of scalpel was being used. Your only care would be about the ability of the person using that tool.

While we are on the subject, let me make a few things clear. Retirement is like a heart procedure in this respect – *the patient wants to get it right the first time*. As we pointed out earlier:

RETIREMENT: IT'S NOT A PLACE. IT'S NOT A COMPANY. IT'S NOT A PRODUCT.

IT'S A PROCESS.

However, this is not a complicated process, and what's really exciting is that the process works. You may already have a firm grasp on the products needed to win the war against mundane and boring retirement. You may know how to wield just the right tools so that your client will not have to live in fear that one of the big five mentioned above will destroy the dream they have been planning for forty years.

You may be able to recite with perfect clarity the products you used to create the income your client so desperately needed. And you may already have helped your client to create a legacy while enjoying the kind of retirement that others can only dream about.

We hope this is true because, just like the surgeon performing the heart procedure, your client is only interested in two things: *How many times have you performed this process – and what is your success rate?*

You may prove to have an incredible success rate. If this is true in your case, then you will never be numbered among those poor souls who definitely need to...

... WAKE UP AND SMELL THE COFFEE.

Chapter Seven:

COMPANY BENEFITS VERSUS PERSONAL BENEFITS

"I owe my soul to the company store."

If you are still with me at this point, we are going to have a lot of fun with this chapter. The subtitle comes from a popular Tennessee Ernie Ford song, "Sixteen Tons," that describes a problem with using a company benefit for coal miners. The benefit that certainly appeared to be a good one allowed the coal miner and his family to purchase almost anything on credit, as long as they purchased the items from the company that employed them. Does this issue sound like something we are dealing with today?

The company provided a very popular benefit the employee certainly needed. Continued use of this benefit, however, left the miner with little control of his future – as indicated in the song title.

Your first thought might be, "What does this have to do with retirement?" I don't want to appear to be condescending, but the answer is that **it has *everything* to do with it.** The benefits provided by your client's company can create a very nice bridge to their retirement. But the misuse of these benefits can place your client in a position where they "owe their souls to the company store."

You may still not be convinced that these two scenarios, separated by so many years, have anything to do with each other. I wasn't even alive during the period when this company store concept was popular, but I think it is safe to say that on the surface, using funds before you made them – if it was the only way you could feed your family – was an extremely prudent decision. I think it is also fair to say that the miner, not to mention his family, was grateful for this benefit. It was the continued use of the benefit, without understanding its long-term cost, that changed the benefit from a godsend to a virtual prison cell. The benefit to the employee was great, but at the same time it had a facet that proved very beneficial to the company.

After all, why do you think they call it a **company** *benefit?*

Let's quickly look at this from another angle: Credit cards don't create problems; the *misuse* and *misunderstanding* of credit cards is what causes the problems. If we're still not tracking together on this comparison between company benefits and credit cards, let's look at it this way: *Credit cards aren't built just to help you. They are designed to make money for the company that offers them.*

A matter of who's in control

The 401(k) is an employee benefit offered by the company that employs them. The continued use of this plan after the employee no longer works for the company can have some adverse affects on the employee, as we have discussed in previous chapters. The company didn't mandate the continued use of the plan any more than the miner had to continue to use the company store. But the retired employee who continues to use the 401(k) can no more dictate the terms and conditions of that document to their company than the miner of yesteryear could dictate to his circumstances.

They each require a personal plan that utilizes company benefits to supply some of their needs, but enables them to determine how and when those benefits will be used. I don't think I have to tell you who will be the one to rescue today's employee from the pitfalls of the company plan. *That would be you!* I don't know enough history to understand who helped the miner, but I am willing to bet it was some outside force. That's why it is so important for you to hold yourself out as the expert, because the corporate employee and the miner didn't intentionally misuse the benefits.

I also want to stress that the companies didn't provide the benefit as a way to hurt the employee. In both cases, the employees simply didn't understand the benefits enough to use them properly. Deciphering benefits wasn't their job. In the case of the corporate employee, it's *your* job; and two people will benefit from your doing it properly – your client and you.

Let's take a look at the world of company benefits and how a personal plan uses the benefits but isn't controlled by them. The 401(k) benefit is one that everyone should take advantage of and it's great that companies provide the plan. The benefit is limited, however, to building a retirement. It has inherent problems when you are trying to live off the 401(k) in retirement. There are drawbacks to this or any other company plan.

No choice vs. multiple choices

In many cases, the plan is limited in the kind of funds one can use in funding their retirement. The plan sponsor usually provides no investment advice to the participant; therefore they have to figure it out on their own. Like many government-sponsored plans, the company plan dictates at what age someone can withdraw money without suffering a tax penalty. By contrast, the employee putting money away outside of the plan has unlimited fund choices, and they can use our expertise on how to use those choices. The employee also is able to decide when they want to retire because they don't have to worry about the tax penalty for early withdrawals.

This is just a warm-up of a company plan versus personal plan comparison. The client becomes the master of the ship, with you as the captain to guide the journey. You will only use the company's plan when it provides the best benefit to your client. In the example we just talked about, where the retiree has built a separate personal plan to supplement the company plan, the retiree would be allowed to use the assets in the personal plan until they reach 60 and then switch over to the company plan, thus avoiding the tax penalty. The client older than 60 who has funds in the bank or a money market fund would still use his personal plan assets first to avoid taxes as long as possible.

You might think this part of the narrative is a waste of your time and just common sense. But I can give you example after example where retired clients would leave 50 or 60 thousand dollars in the bank while they paid the government taxes on the money they spent out of the company plan. They had a mindset that the money in the bank was their security blanket for their retirement plan, when in fact that's what the IRA should have been. They misused the company plan, from the standpoint of the IRS and tax liability.

They didn't receive any advice to help them understand that the bank money should be spent first. They had been told to leave the company money alone and use your savings while you are still working. They thought that when you retired you were then to use the retirement money, because no one told them that it is still the last place to go for extra money since it's taxable.

When you look at all the taxes they paid, you could truly say they reached the point where they *owed their soul to the company store.* There are no advantages to the 401(k) after the employee has left the company, so at that time you need to roll it into an IRA and dictate the use of the personal retirement plan first.

Knowing how best to use their money

There are also many individuals who believe now that they are retired they should use the retirement monies to pay cash for tangible goods, such as a car. Paying cash for a car is a good thing if there is extra money in the bank, but pulling it out of their retirement account would make the taxes too high. The money in the retirement account will provide your client several more years of income if this error in judgment does not occur.

Remember: The company benefit did not create the problem; *the misuse of the benefit is what creates the problem.* The company benefits do not come with a manual instructing how to use them.

If there is any advice at all to given by the company, that advice ceases when the employee retires. This timing, of course, is terrible because just when they need advice on how to properly use the benefits, it's no longer available!

That's why they have you – and that's why it is important to craft them a personal plan to fill in the gaps of the company plan. The 401(k) concept was implemented years ago as a company benefit to help the client save money for retirement. It had specific penalties built into it to discourage the employee from using it early. However, it was never meant to be the only retirement savings provision, and it certainly was never intended to stay with the company after the employee retired. So the retiree needs you to help with the personal plan and proper displacement from the 401(k). The very nature of this company benefit and its non-company counterpart, as we have described it, is the way they were meant to be used from the start.

We have worked over the 401(k), so now let's concentrate on those companies that still employ the use of a pension. This benefit is a dying breed, and most companies have already eliminated it for new employees. However, it's not a dying breed because it didn't help the employee. It's a dying breed because it cost the company too much to administer. It remains tremendously important to your potential retiree because it creates *income.*

But let's suppose the individual you are working with has been working for this company for thirty years and has this benefit available to him. The pension plan can be a valuable part of his retirement plan if used correctly. So we need to make sure that the client does use his options properly.

As we previously discussed, the client needs to take the biggest payout possible. This will allow him to supplement the rest of his need for income with monies that were moved from the 401(k). We will have to back up this plan by buying life insurance to protect the pension. What about the life insurance they had at work? That insurance is almost always cancelled when the employee retires.

Remember it's a company plan, not a personal one, and your client is no longer working for that company.

Captives to the company plan

The reason it gets cancelled underscores the main point of this entire chapter. It's company insurance. It's a company plan. *It's not your client's, it is the company's.* The employee can't control how it gets offered, how much is offered, or when it goes away. But if they buy the insurance outside the company, they can. They have the same product, but now it has become a personal benefit.

There is no comparison between company benefits and personal benefits, and you are the individual offering the personal ones. You will win this contest hands down. You just have to make the client understand how it works.

When it comes to life insurance, this is especially important. Just when a person arrives at the age where the mortality tables indicate a higher chance of dying, they no longer have life insurance through their company. The only way to keep the company life insurance is to work for the company until they die. Need I say it again? *They owe their soul to the company store.*

You also want to make sure that if the company pension has a Social Security income rider that it only be used if it provides a bridge to Social Security. If the retiree is close to Social Security age, chances are very good this is not a rider they want to take. You are the person who helps them decide when and how all these benefits fit. The company plan is a one-size-fits-all plan. You, on the other hand, measure each benefit carefully to get just the right fit.

One size doesn't fit all

The level income benefit can be a godsend to a 50-year-old retiree. He or she will at 50 years old have ten years of extra pension. This would afford them the ability not to touch their IRA, which if used would cost them a ten percent tax penalty. It is exactly the additional monies they needed to make an early exit from their company. The use of this benefit for the 50-year-old made all the difference in the world. Without your counsel, they might have turned it down and worked ten more years on a job they couldn't stand.

The same benefit, however, can be a real detriment to a 61-year-old retiree. They would find themselves giving too much of their pension away. They should have counted the cost, but had never been shown how to understand it – because it was a *company plan*. They now find themselves, through misuse of what for some is an outstanding company benefit, in the unenviable position of *owing their soul to the company store.*

You can help the employee build a personal retirement plan similar to the 401(k) in investment makeup, but funded with after-tax dollars. This allows them to avoid pitfalls years after retirement. When the client is Social Security age, there are limits to how much this individual can take out of the IRA without giving some of the Social Security money back to the government. There are no limits of this kind, however, when the retiree draws the money from a personal retirement plan funded with after-tax dollars. They may have been retired for years, but you are still helping them to make sure the company benefits are used properly.

There are many examples on record where a unknowing retiree pulled three or four thousand dollars out of their IRA and never realized – until it was too late – this was going to cost them more than that amount in lost Social Security funds. You are the person that saved them from being caught in the same trap of the miners of old. You kept them from being in the unenviable position of *owing their soul to the company store.*

The health care dilemma

Speaking of items that occur years after retirement, most company health insurance plans keep increasing in cost. That will have the poor retiree spending more and more of his retirement dollars for health care costs instead of spending it for a round of golf or a special vacation trip. Retirees need to know about Medicare and the supplements associated with Medicare – and that isn't a company plan. It is, once again, a personal plan. The correct use of this supplement, as well as several other forms of the Medicare plan, will allow retirees the freedom to enjoy their retirement in ways the company health care plan could never have provided.

We dare not underestimate the value of the company plan, so we must understand it. There are many cases where just a few more months at work before retiring would allow the retiree a bigger co-payment by their employer. The employee may be ready to leave, but they could be coaxed to stay a few more months if that is what you advise. This might be a hard call for you, because you depend on retirement monies that will provide your commissions. But if it's the right call, you must make it.

This might seem like you are encouraging them to owe their soul to the company store. This simply isn't the case. The extra insurance cost savings will be liberating for them in their future retirement years. Don't think they won't want to mention this to their friends. Nothing like a satisfied customer!

Without this much-needed advice, and with continued utilization of the company health plan as a one-size-fits-all idea, the retiree could find himself even more of a slave to the company than the miners of old. There are many examples today of much older retirees going back to the workplace. And it's not because they wanted to, but simply because they thought they had to – because of the health insurance.

You and I provide options, and don't ever forget: *Americans want options.* The benefits the company offers are good *if* the client has someone to help him understand how these benefits can be used in a personal retirement plan. That "someone" is you.

You are the one that can make sure the children of a client inherit the money originally invested in the 401(k) – because you moved it to an IRA. You are the person that let the client pass their pension to their children when the company plan wouldn't allow this – because you backed the pension with life insurance. You are the one who made sure that the employee used the level income Social Security benefit when it fit their circumstances. You are the one that made sure that the client didn't draw so much out of their retirement plan they had to give back part of the Social Security proceeds that they had been paying into for years.

You were able to insure that their Social Security wasn't compromised because you helped them build a personal set of investments that didn't count against the Social Security wage rate when it was used. You are the one that made sure the client understood the retirement dollars were intended to protect their retirement, not for use as a lump sum spending pool.

Voice of reason ... or no voice at all

In other words, you were the voice of reason. There is no voice at all in the company plan. You are the person who frees them from self-imposed slavery. You are the one who helps them see that the dream they had of retirement can actually be realized – because you fit all the pieces into just the right slots. You, and you alone, are the one who put them in a position where they will never, ever *owe their soul to the company store.*

The company was not at fault in any of these examples. It was the way the benefit was being improperly used that created the problem. The way the problem was alleviated was not through the use of some special product, such as life insurance or a certain placement of stock or a CD in the portfolio. The issues were resolved by the *proper use* of the benefits.

Think of it this way: The company that produces a certain breathing apparatus is not the cause for the patient dying on the operating table. The person attending to and using that particular product is generally the cause of the death. Can you imagine how insane it would be to have no one attending to this device at all because the patient decided that it was the device that would keep them alive? This is the way many retirees approach retirement.

They feel if they can just find the right product, maybe they can do it themselves.

YOU (or someone like you) *need to tell them the truth*. And that truth is that you can build a retirement without a lot of help, but managing it after you no longer have a job is a dangerous thing to do without help. ***They don't – and won't – get any help from the company store.***

I probably don't need to tell you that if you are going to fill that role, you must be hired because you know how to use the scalpel, rather than being hired because you are licensed to hold one. This makes you wonder what would have happened if you had been available way back then and had the kind of knowledge about the miners' credit issues that you have about today's retirement benefits.

You just have to wonder if "Ole Ern" – Tennessee Ernie Ford – would have ever had the material to sing that song!

Chapter Eight:

THE IMPORTANCE OF MANAGING YOUR BASE

"Go with what brought you"

The phrase, *"Go With What Brought You,"* is not something that gives the listener the impression you have mastered the English language and therefore are able to wield its magic better than most people. The meaning, even though perhaps it sounds a bit hickish, is understood by most people. It simply means maintaining the principles that helped you reach this point in your life. It's perfect for this chapter because the title indicates we are trying to maintain the business and clients we have previously established.

We learned how to capture the retirement market in the previous chapters. We looked at the basic needs for staffing to continue building, and we have talked about using a very good referral system to increase our base. But I have not had much to say about maintaining the clients we already have until now. We want to grow, but also have to keep the foundation we started with to give us something to build on.

The way we do that is: *Go with what brought you.* The client base was built because the prospects were impressed with the amount of interest you showed in them when other planners were only talking to their wealthy friends. We are going to step that up a notch and show them we aren't just interested in the sale that made them a client. We are interested in preserving the relationship we established with them.

Nothing has changed

That's the premise the relationship was built on, and you are going to show them that this is only the beginning: You still are the person you seemed to be when they first met you. You are going to help with all their needs. Nothing has changed – you are still just as interested in them as when you first met. This is *going with what brought you,* and this is the concept that will help you to *manage your base.*

As the saying goes, "Don't just talk about it – *do* something about it!" We have certainly talked enough about this principle, so let's continue the journey by actually doing something about the issue.

The ongoing, sustained contact I mentioned in earlier chapters is the ticket, and it will be used to keep our base of clients in perfect health. In my practice, I make a point to get in front of my clients as often as possible. I have the clients come in to pick up their contract when I could have mailed it to them. I have them journey to our office for their annual update even though that same task could have been performed over the phone or by email.

The personal contact was what I used to earn their business in the first place. And it is that same quality I will use to maintain their business. For instance, I need to ask them about their will – or their lack of one. I need to verify what impact their aging parents will have on their lives. I need to ensure that their Social Security benefits are not compromised by the amount of money they are taking out of their individual retirement account.

There are many other points that need to be covered in order for me to continue being the person the client hired. They hired someone that would manage their retirement, and all I have to do to reassure them that they didn't hire the wrong person is simply – *go with what brought you.*

Does this mean that you are never going to change anything? On the contrary, you want to utilize change as your ally. The thing you don't change is the person they hired. They don't want that person to change, because that's the person who painted for them the dream of a perfect retirement. So the way you manage the base is simple: keep painting.

You started with a rough draft that was the retirement module, then moved on to rolling their retirement funds and protecting their pension with life insurance. This allowed the portrait to become more detailed. We have now reached a point where they have been retired for some time, and the picture for them has to reflect this change.

Digging deeper during updates

Your update meetings will take on a whole new character. You are going to dig much deeper: For instance, are they inheriting anything in the future? Is the estate properly secured? Has the issue of long-term care been properly reviewed?

The answer to these and many more questions is also the equation enabling you to *maintain your base,* and of course all you and I are doing is *going with what brought you.* The most common statement made by a spouse before a divorce is, "you are not the person I married." We don't want our client to divorce us. To make sure that does not happen, we will need to provide the stability that keeps the relationship going.

We have already mentioned in previous chapters that this relationship provides a strong referral source. However, we have not discussed until now the new business that is created from the same relationship. We find that a good size base, well-maintained, can create 30% of your new business. That's right – I didn't say "renewal business." I said *new business.* We can't afford the divorce. We have to *maintain the base.*

The new business and what takes place to maintain the base are one and the same. You must ensure that long-term care issues are handled. That means you are selling, or you are teamed with a financial professional who is selling, long-term care. You are ensuring that extra reserves are not just sitting in the bank, which of course means that as the years go by, you are investing more than their 401(k). You are making sure that some provision is made for the grandchildren's education if your client has an interest in this area, and that means you are doing college funds.

These items and many others will be byproducts of a well-performed annual review. This review will also place you in a position of working with the adult children and/or the aging parents of your clients. You will earn these opportunities by either providing advice on things such as estate planning, or providing them with a source that can offer the needed counsel. You will also find yourself involved in helping them with the areas of planned giving and endowments.

These things were not part of the original retirement conversation, but they are all an essential part of *maintaining your base.* There are so many avenues of new business that can arise during the annual review that we have only scratched the surface. The older retired client may need a Medicare supplement. The younger retired client might wish to try their hand at individual stocks, as well as some forms of options trading.

The possibilities are limitless. Remember, it is all part of the equation for *maintaining the base.* The very things that we are excited about doing because they create new commissions are also what we must do to ensure that we don't find ourselves divorced from our clients.

Always strengthening the bond

This isn't all we do. There are many items that we must help with that don't immediately pay you, but they are also essential to *maintain the base.* This is in no way a departure from what we did in the beginning of this relationship. We explained company benefits to the bewildered prospective retiree, knowing full well that in itself, this did not create a commission. When we fast-forward this issue, we may well find ourselves giving advice on what to do with land and businesses with respect to estate planning, which in itself will not produce new commissions. But the good news is that these types of issues, as well as so many more, create a retirement bond that is not easily broken.

You are performing work for which you may not receive compensation, which means the relationship was always built on trust. You showed them the way, but didn't charge until they accepted the advice.

There are so many minor issues in retirement that can turn into major issues. A very good example of this involves a retired individual wanting to use retirement dollars to purchase a new car. The review you perform to help them understand that this is not a good idea will not create commissions; however, it will strengthen the relationship between you and your client. And that, in many cases, is worth its weight in gold.

This was the basis of your relationship from the very beginning. You were the person that opened their eyes to the difference between the company benefit and a personal benefit. You are the one that opened their eyes and helped them see just how great retirement can be, so that should include helping them see that buying the car with pretax dollars makes Uncle Sam smile and hurts their plan.

Continuing the ongoing journey

You are continuing the journey you started together at the very beginning of your relationship. You helped them navigate rolling their 401(k), and now you may be helping them get a Medicare supplement. You will be helping them turn their excess funds into a trust for the grandkids before you know it. You also helped them do many of the same things with their parents' estate, just before they lost their loved ones to the fate that awaits all of us.

You were the one who helped their children set up their retirement benefits in a way that the parents would have done, if only they had known you at that age. You are rewriting their story, doing it one chapter at a time. This whole process, for which you are being paid, is simply a part of *maintaining your base.* You are performing all these new functions, but it is part of the same proven principle that you repeat again and again: You are just *going with what brought you!*

It's really a simple equation: We are born, grow up, get jobs, get married, have a family, grow old, retire, and die. We all want to think during the time between birth and death that we made some difference. We all would like to think that at our funeral there is a consensus among those in attendance that we succeeded at making the most of our lives. That we made good choices, and as a result of those choices many lives, including our own, were made better.

You and I are granted a small fragment of someone's life, and we are now helping them work through the choices they must make. We are a part of their dream, and we can have a role – a portion of the responsibility – for the difference they made or did not make in life. We are not responsible for the life insurance they didn't buy if we presented it to them. But we are responsible for creating some of those choices. It becomes partly our responsibility to help ensure that the comments made at their funeral are good ones.

Helping in a way that makes a difference

The cycle continues from generation to generation, and that's how we *maintain the base.* We never want to lose our way and discover that we have changed and didn't help the story end as well as it could have, simply because we might not get paid for the advice. That is not at all how we started; that certainly isn't *going with what brought you.*

If we should become so shallow in our thinking and allow ourselves to fall into this pit, then we don't deserve the base we have, nor should we be allowed to maintain it. But it is a wondrous thing to observe a life that is lived in such a way that the world truly is a better place because the person was there. It is just as exciting to play a role in that life, and the monetary benefit we receive sometimes pales in comparison to the feeling you gain from knowing you have played a small part in the life of an individual who made a difference.

It's all a continuation of the same fairytale in the new and exciting land of retirement. You will help them avoid the dragons that can swallow the retiree whole and destroy the dream that they started with. You will be the calming force when the stock market tumbles – or CD rates fall – and it appears that a tornado has spun them into a land distant from the one they imagined when they began the retirement journey. You will protect them from the turns in the road that would allow taxes to eat up their future income, just as the seven dwarfs protected Snow White.

You will allow them to pass down a better life for their children, just as Cinderella's father desired for her and her fairy godmother provided. Remember the rollover that you did and the advice that you gave concerning their benefits in the very beginning of your relationship? It was just that – a beginning.

The future of their retirement hangs in the balance, and as is true in any fairy tale, this can have either a happy ending or a tragic one. Do you want to know how to *maintain your base?* The answer is sprinkled with fairy dust. You simply have to *GO WITH WHAT BROUGHT YOU* – and that always makes the ending a happy one!

Chapter Nine:

HOW TO TRANSITION INTO A TEAM CONCEPT

There is no "I" in T-E-A-M

Teamwork: This is probably the most effective concept – other than our review of how retirement works – that we will discuss. In reality, this is the most important arrow in your quiver, but it is also the hardest one to keep on target. The overall problem involves differences in personalities, and therein lies the crux of the issue.

We have discussed concepts up to this point, but personalities didn't factor into our discussion of those ideas. We have generally explained the need for a team, and have expressed the view that you can't build your practice by yourself. But we haven't discussed the fine points of how to accomplish this.

The subtitle of this chapter can be very misleading for many readers because when you hear the words, *"There is not 'I' in TEAM,"* you are challenging yourself to live up to that statement. It is not difficult to manage yourself; it is the team players that you must find a way to manage. And the more success the team has, the harder it will be to manage that team.

We have talked about building the retirement base one company at a time. You can obviously increase the number of companies you work with much faster if there are several of you finding them. The synergy of a team can be unbelievable, and when you are working together in harmony, you will begin to move at warp speed. When that starts happening, you need to congratulate the other players, even though they are being adequately compensated. You also have to ensure that the new company is a part of the overall team's success, and that it doesn't become the sole property of the financial professional who worked their way into that company.

You have to become someone who can impart the wisdom of *there is no "I" in TEAM* without actually communicating those words in the form of a threat to your teammates. This is a fine line to walk, but the rewards are immense. You are the manager, but you are also a player. The other players have to be convinced that they must have you in both positions and that they won't achieve as much success by themselves.

Finders, Minders and Grinders

I want to make sure we are on the same page about the possible personality conflicts that can occur. The financial world is made up of "finders," "minders," and "grinders." Just in case the terms aren't familiar to you, let me give you some quick definitions:

The "finder" is the person with the great personality. He or she has never met a stranger. They can fill a conference room with prospects and not even break a sweat. The good news is that they enjoy doing it. What they are *not* excited about, however, is completing a lot of messy paperwork. They tend to describe things in generalities; though general in nature, they leave the prospective client with a beautiful picture of retirement.

The "minder," on the other hand, enjoys making sure everyone is in the right place at the right time. They schedule the update meetings, and prepare the file for those updates to make certain that everything can and will be covered. They send out cards or remind you to call on a client's birthday. They ensure the premiums are paid on time for any product you sell. The best part of all this is that they love doing this kind of work, but would never want to prospect for clients. They just want to take care of the existing clients.

The last category is the "grinder." It's the last category, but certainly not the least in importance. They take care of all the paperwork, and they love completing applications, pumping out illustrations, and creating a vivid picture on paper. They are not good with words, and typically do not enjoy striking up conversations with prospects, but their attention to detail on the paperwork is to die for!

As you might guess, these three positions are not interchangeable. Each one of them thinks with full assurance that they have the perfect job and would rather not change jobs with the other two. And that's exactly as you want it to be.

You can captain a group where you are the only finder because the minders and grinders don't want to do your job. It is possible to have an "I" in TEAM and not have it become a problem area with grinders and minders. But this would mean you are not reaching the full potential, because you have a small group and you function as the boss, not the captain.

Keeping the focus on the TEAM

A very good minder and grinder can handle several finders, and there's a need to have several finders to feed the team. This is where we find the personality problems, because these people are to the financial world what wide receivers are to football. They are the individuals that will try all they can to insert the "I" into TEAM. You need to have them, and they need you. But it is hard to keep them in line, and they have a tendency to want to make it *their* team instead of *THE* team.

You started the team, and it is now moving at warp speed. Certain members of the team can be endowed with selective memory and may on occasion think it was they that started the team. The evolution that takes place to get the whole team in place can make it very difficult to keep the simple word "I" out of the team.

We are going to start with building the team, and then we will come back to the part about managing it. The first ingredients you should add to your team are the minders and grinders. I think you will have a lot more success if all of these individuals either are, or have been, financial professionals themselves. This cuts down on the training because they are presently doing this kind of work or have done it in the past.

You can start out by using administrative types that you train, but you want to quickly transfer to better performers as soon as you can find the right person. I don't know anyone that has the market cornered on how to find good talent. I do know, however, if you have begun implementing the process we discussed in the first eight chapters, these individuals will be seeking you just as much as you are seeking them.

Finding the ideal grinder or minder

The perfect person to be your grinder or minder is that individual who hasn't quite made their mark as a financial professional. They lacked nothing when it came to technical abilities and work ethic; they just never became comfortable with calling prospects. They can make your system work, and together you are unbeatable.

This probably goes without saying, but you are choosing them to do this kind of work because they are good at it. You might not readily admit it, but they are better at doing this work than you are. Therefore you should avoid any attempt to micromanage them. You simply create the system; they will make it sing.

The incentive for their activity level should always be based on the team results, *not a set salary*. This means if the team does poorly, so do they; the opposite is also true. There should never be a limit on what they can earn. If a limit is set, two things are taking place – and both are bad.

The first is that you have put a limit to how much of the team's success one of the team members can experience. The second effect is even worse. *YOU* and nobody but *YOU* have just inserted the letter "I" into TEAM. *It does not belong there.* The more comfortable your team becomes with the arrangement in which everyone shares in their success, the more likely they are to help with the work of finding business.

Not always easy to identify

When you reach this point, you are able to start looking for a person that has your ability to find prospects, but lacks your vision for the overall team. They are stars in their own right, but *without your vision they won't shine very brightly.*

These individuals are the hardest to find because no one has a fail-safe formula for spotting success before it happens. There is a popular Christian song that states, "You will know they are Christians by their love." This song makes it sound as if these people are easy to pick out, but that may not always be the case. The concept of finding someone that is able to help you build your retirement business by bringing in new clients is even harder to describe. The candidate will not be readily identified as a result of their sex, ethnic origin, age, or previous work experiences.

I am sorry if this seems an impossible task, but I can give you one really strong clue since you have already made the business work and now you want it to work better: Look for someone *just like you.* You will enjoy the honeymoon, and business will grow dramatically if you can find this person.

This is just like the rest of the concepts we have discussed: If you want to find them, then you will. Why did I say that you will *enjoy the honeymoon?* It's very simple: Long-term success isn't guaranteed. At first, he or she is enamored with you and your existing staff; then they begin to wonder about one thing or another, and the synergy can suffer. I didn't say the synergy necessarily *will* suffer, but it can.

You have to be able to spot this sickness the minute it starts and be prepared to cure it. It can take different forms. They can wonder about the systems you have in place, so you should be open to change. However, you aren't open to changing just to pacify them. You want to be open to change because you are a *team*, and a good idea should be used to improve the team no matter who thought of it.

Wide receivers don't fire quarterbacks

They might be less than excited about other team members, and this issue is harder to deal with. To again use a football analogy, *you can't let the wide receiver fire the quarterback.* The most common dilemma, however, could be *you* and their desire to take over your position. That is an area where you obviously can give no ground. You have to manage in such a way that they can realize the only way they can achieve that status is to spend the years you have already spent to make these concepts work.

This approach is usually a winner because most of them are too impatient to start over. As a result, the team dodges a major bullet. The concept is ideal because everyone has a bad game now and then, and in this case the team still wins because it is not dependent on the performance of any single individual. It also means that if a starter is out on vacation, the game still goes on. At the same time, the individual taking the vacation has a worry-free situation – all because they didn't try to put an "I" in TEAM.

You can really start to feel the momentum in these cases, and nothing can bind a team together like momentum. The prospective clients get to hear a mini-sermon on how many of you there are at work on their case and how you are all committed to the same goal. You are unbeatable because there are so many of you.

At most of the other places a prospective client visits there will be only one financial professional working on the case. You need to capitalize on this advantage. Mention it and make certain that the clients understand it, because it's true. One single player can't beat several players in any sport and, similarly, one financial professional can't possibly offer what your team can provide a prospect.

The point we just made was about numbers, but it's better than that because *each of you is a specialist.* The prospect is faced with two undeniable, very positive situations: There are several of you, and you are all specialists. And the best thing of all is, the fees for the client are the same.

Make sure that you point these facts out. You are managing a team and dealing with numerous personalities. You are taking a commissions risk to do it. You cannot assume the prospect understands the advantages they would be receiving. *You have to make sure to underscore this important point.*

Because there are so many of you on the team, you can come at a case from many different directions. You can insert fresh players into the game because you have strength and versatility in numbers. You can enjoy the success as mentioned earlier as a group – and that's a lot more fun.

Take others with you to the pinnacle

Do you want to reach the pinnacle of success? Then take my advice: Take other people with you and you will reach it. You need to vary your presentations by utilizing the best each team member has to offer. You need to have different players studying different products you could use so that the combined group can come up with the best alternative for each situation.

You need one person preparing the seller for a presentation, and the next time alternate the positions so another team member is doing the preparation. Continue to do this until you get the perfect winning combination. The whole process makes you so versatile that it almost seems unbelievable how easy it is to gain new work.

Make sure you use the whole team in the process, because it is essential that you all feel like the increased sales have come as a result of the team. This is one of the hardest parts to pull off. If you don't do it smoothly, you will soon have a player trying to put that "I" into TEAM. And I can't state it more strongly or more often: *There isn't one!*

The problem with the "I" is that it begins to break up the synergy – and that can cause the team to break. You have to continually remind and reinforce for the team, just as you did for the prospect, that you are good at what you do because there are many of you. You have to tell them that if word gets out into the retiree community that there is split in this group, then the momentum will be lost.

Your clients should – and need to – see you as a family. They have attended functions with the whole family. They have talked about different aspects of their retirement with each individual player. There is no way you can take that family apart without it having a significant effect on your team's base. You know this is true, and you had better make sure the team knows it also. Your communication on this point isn't a threat to any one individual on the team. ***It's just a fact.***

Team meetings: The necessary glue

The glue that helps to hold things together will be your team meetings. I know some of us hate these meetings; this is because, we reason, if we weren't in these meetings we would be selling. However, each meeting is a crucial time, greatly needed for holding the team together. Communication and trust are the most important factors in sales. This is also true of a good team. It is essential that we are effectively communicating and interacting on our group goals at least on a weekly basis.

Abraham Lincoln made this observation that we can apply to the importance of meetings and planning: "Should I be given a timetable to cut a certain amount of wood and it was of paramount importance that I cut as much as possible during this period of time, I would spend the biggest majority of the time given me sharpening my axe." This came from a pioneer who was well-acquainted with cutting wood – and getting the job done properly and efficiently.

These meetings will keep us on the same page with the clients we are trying to help, and will keep us plugged in with each other as well. We have to talk regularly or the "marriage" begins to suffer. It needs to be understood that none of us has worked this hard, or invested this much energy, just to have the organization break up. These meetings will make the organization much stronger because it is a time to air out our differences and then get back to the business of helping our prospective clients retire.

There are things you can't change or replace individually, no matter how good you are. For instance, you can't make yourself older or younger. Both the client who wants youth and the one who wants years of experience can get it in one team, but they can't get it in one person. The client who wants an analyst and the one who wants someone burning with passion can't get it in the same body. *It has to be a TEAM.* The Eagles are a legendary singing group, but only because they are The *Eagles.* The music wouldn't work nearly as well if it were just The Eagle.

Once you have established yourself at a particular company as the team that can help with retirement, it becomes very difficult to be as effective if the team breaks up. Inevitably, you are going to suffer casualties as individuals decide to spread their wings. So when this occurs, what should you do? You just have to go out and get a replacement. That's what you need to do to keep the system running well; even the renegade with the newfound knowledge can't be very competitive because they forgot the secret: *There is no "I" in TEAM.*

The only real danger of losing the edge you have established is if *YOU personally* forget that secret. It won't work as well for the person who leaves the team – and it won't work as well for you if you get discouraged, decide it isn't worth the effort and try to go solo. It's much sweeter to share success than to be a loner. Who are you going to celebrate with if you are the only person involved in the process?

In the Bible we find a beautiful description of this teamwork principle: "Two are better than one, because they have a good return for their work. If one falls down, his friend can help him up. But pity the man who falls and has no one to help him up! Also, if two lie down together, they will keep warm. But how can one keep warm alone? Though one may be overpowered, two can defend themselves. A cord of three strands is not quickly broken" (Ecclesiastes 4:9-12).

Good for future generations

The process is a cycle. It's good for your clients, it's good for you, and it's good for the next generation. Just like the person who took time to do estate planning so that future generations can be blessed, you are sharing a secret that will bless future generations of financial professionals.

You might be able to spot the next great talent who will make a difference in the lives of people you will never meet. Granted, you might not have done it for that reason. You may have done it because you read this book and thought you could be more success-ful as a group than you could be individually. (Make no mistake: That assumption was exactly correct.) You may have just wanted to transition into a team. Regardless, the motivational factor isn't important. What *is* important is the result.

And that result is you built a team that changed things for the better. That change would have been impossible to perform by just one individual. You might not have known the secret when you started; all you wanted to do was build a team. However, the end result was so much better.

You are going to make your knowledge bless so many more lives because you shared it. You are going to help others to build their own teams because you shared with them. You are going to elimi-nate the errors that retirees make in locations where you don't even live – because you shared. The whole system is going to be so much better because you placed yourself at risk trying to help another financial professional.

You may well start a movement that changes the face of the industry, and movements are never singular. ***You kept the "I" out of TEAM and as a result, many people were helped in many ways.*** You can't beat that feeling!

Chapter Ten:

RUNNING A MATURE RETIREMENT BUSINESS

It just doesn't get any better than this!

There is no such thing as reaching a point of "having it made" in this business, but as your business matures it might seem like that is just what's happening. The truth of the matter is, after years of taking care of people in retirement, you have now reached the point that they are taking care of you. The referrals are almost on autopilot, so there is now a steady stream of new folks that you are working with. The staff is taking care of many of the things you found so difficult to do in the beginning. You have created passion for helping retirees, and you're beginning to find that many of the things that helped to build the business are becoming much easier to accomplish.

Remember the line from an earlier chapter: *Go with what brought you.* You don't have to spend as much time as you once did to build the business, so you have to maximize your time using the trait that started it all, the trait you must always continue to use: ***You have to spend your days demonstrating that you really care about your clients.***

You always made time for it, but now you have time to do it even better. You need to ask about the rest of the family when you perform an update. You need to make sure that if any part of your staff is having a problem of any sort, you are there to help them. The mature practice simply means that you are practicing maturity – and that means you are concentrating on the other members of your team so much that you have lost the focus on yourself.

Moving from 'need to do it' to 'want to do it'

This concept is like so many other things we have developed. You do it at first because you need to, so that the business will become better. But then you continue to do it in the long run because you want to do it. When you reach the point where it becomes just a natural part of your day, that is the time when you will be able to truly say, *"It just doesn't get any better than this!"*

The business is mature because you are mature, and don't think the word won't get around. You now go to funerals not because you are expected to be there, but because you lost someone who was close to you. These people stood by you when you had no credentials but yourself, and now you are standing beside their loved ones when they can't be there themselves to help.

The athlete that excels is the one that can make the big play because it became natural. They didn't think about it, they just executed. You won't worry about what one part of the team is earning because all you care about is how the team performs. You aren't trying to measure how much you make from each client meeting; rather, you are thinking about how much you can help. The ironic thing about it is this: You won't be worrying about how much you make off the meeting – and that's the very time you will probably make the most.

I think you're getting the picture. The mature practice is one where each player is concerned so much about the clients they are servicing that they don't have time to worry about themselves. This needs to take place in every position on your team. You won't have to tell your clients that is how you feel, because they will notice it. This behavior spreads fast, and there is nothing better to spread than good will.

Heart of a mature practice

You really do have it made at this point because it is so rewarding to help others. This makes them want to help you – and they will. This is the heart of a mature practice. You're not telling them how good that you and your staff are; instead, you have redoubled your efforts to make them understand how much they mean to you.

The individuals you built your business around would much rather talk about themselves than hear about you. It's important for them to tell you during their reviews what is new in their lives. They may have inherited some funds or started a business in their retirement years. We know one thing for sure: It won't help them and won't make you any money to talk about yourself, but the future is unlimited if you will just *listen*.

Again, you need to *go with what brought you* – and what brought you was *listening*. They don't want to hear about you, they simply want you and me to appreciate them. Affirmation is one the strongest emotions in existence. We all crave it, and you as the team leader need to be shoveling it out in buckets.

There is no greater feeling than that of helping someone else. Living out the statement, "It is better to give than to receive," is the sure sign of a mature retirement practice. You might hear a prospective client moan from time to time about how a financial professional talked too much about himself or herself, but you will never hear someone complain about a financial professional talking too much about the prospect and their needs.

Time for experimentation

You can afford to experiment at this point by giving the players on your team the opportunity to try to perform functions that aren't in their normal scope of work. The "grinder," during his or her extra hours, can try their hand at being a "finder." They may become successful and if so, reward them for it. This part of the work has become easier at this point because the size of the client base has grown so the grinder isn't taking as big a step as they would have been a few years ago. They are calling people they already know rather than cold calling.

Your practice might find that just keeping up with the reviews will lead you into areas that you didn't foresee. For instance, you may discover that a widow whose husband you worked with finds a new mate, perhaps a widower, and there is a great deal of new work your team needs to perform in the process. This was not an account that you had to cold call for – it's simply the result of a mature retirement business continuing to perform for the folks that put their trust in it.

You had no idea when you helped the now-deceased client to retire years before that you would one day be servicing a whole new family as a result of that relationship. We see these situations being repeated in our practice over and over again. Believe me, *it just doesn't get any better than this.*

However, without the team interacting in the lives of the whole family, you might not have reached this point. Your relationship was with the now-deceased retiree. Your team, on the other hand, had developed a strong bond with the rest of his family. The future earnings were based more on your team's success.

Without each of you and your individual talents, the relationship might have died with the client. You're not the one the wife called to check on her husband's monthly check. That call was made to your business manager. The initial commissions were created because of your abilities and talents. But the future commissions, without question, were garnered because of the team's talents and abilities, proving once again that it is costly to everyone if anyone tries to put an "I" in TEAM.

Temptation to 'label' clients

Now we are going to take a quick stroll down the negative or opposite side of this situation, and it is a temptation for anyone with a mature practice to take for granted what you already have.

When this happens, we start trying to "label" the clients we service. This is the road more often traveled by our peers in the industry, but it's definitely one you don't want spend any time on.

This tendency starts out harmlessly enough. Perhaps just one person in your staff notices there doesn't seem to be a lot to the client's portfolio, and maybe there's not much to review on a yearly basis, so why not just skip it? But think about it for a moment: What if they did that to you? What if they won some large settlement, but didn't say anything to you because you didn't call them in for their review? How would you know – if you didn't do the review?

We have noticed that some of the largest cases we have closed this year resulted from clients that appeared to have very little additional to offer to our organization. Nevertheless, we just did what we always have done – conducted the annual review anyway – without any thought that it could work out the way it did.

Why *wouldn't* we do the review? It didn't take much of our time. This is so much easier than the way you started this business. The time expended now, versus the rewards, is inconceivably small compared to the way it was when you were first starting out.

This is the point in your career when you need to take advantage of opportunities that were never presented to you before. Suppose Jane Doe is retiring from XYZ Company and she wants you to come to her retirement party. Can you believe it? You never were invited to something like this before, so you go and provide a cookie bouquet or gift. It turns out that you and your staff member who goes with you end up being introduced to the twenty other prospects that are present.

When you get back to the office, you discover you've already received a call from a prospect and you call to set the meeting. You learn during the call that the prospect got your name from someone who was in the office for a discovery meeting last week. You got a referral from someone who isn't even a client yet! I can't help it – I have to say again, *it just doesn't get any better than this.*

Always sticking with the fundamentals

The whole thing comes back to fundamentals. You were fishing in the right place – the retirement market – and the news got around fast that someone was doing this work. You aren't just a specialist: You're a specialist at the right time and the right place – kind of like a pediatrician practicing during the middle of the Baby Boom.

Everyone needs your services, and because the practice is mature, more and more folks are finding out about you and your company. You have hired the staff to cover the increased demand, and you also have other retirement specialists to assist with the prospecting calls. Did we mention that prospecting calls are coming a lot easier these days?

This is all because you continue to take advantage of a secret. What secret? The secret is that there is an extraordinary amount of people retiring at this time. You have known and exploited that fact for years, and yet it must still be a secret or there would be a lot of other financial professionals working in this market.

January 1, 2011, the experts tell us, was a milestone date. Some are even calling it "the day of reckoning." That was the day that the first official "Baby Boomers," individuals born on January 1, 1946, turned 65. Since that date, every single day 10,000 Baby Boomers on average are reaching the age of 65, and that rate will continue for the next 19 years. So there's ample time to engage in what we've been talking about between now and December 31, 2029!

Despite these intriguing facts, it continues to be a "secret" because there are only a handful of planners working in this area. We are very happy with this situation, however, because it means more clients for us with less effort. We are finally getting calls from prospects. Yes, they are now calling us, and as amazing as it sounds, very few if any financial professionals are making any attempt to cut in on the party.

This is almost unbelievable: As I said, the prospects are calling *YOU*, and yet most financial professionals aren't interested. These same individuals would be highly motivated to spend thousands in advertising costs if they had even a remote belief that one million-aire businessman would eventually call them. However, they won't because millionaires in general don't flock. They just won't adver-tise for you (putting in a good word on your behalf to friends) no matter how happy you make them. By comparison, the common worker or his widowed bride will, in fact, do this kind of advertis-ing. Simply because they are so pleased with how you have served them, and they know their friends would be pleased as well.

The machine is starting to run itself. You are at the head of a movement that will follow the Boomer to and through his or her retirement, and there are very few making an effort to unseat you. It sounds almost too good to be true, but you bought into this issue 10 years ago when many other financial professionals felt it wasn't an area they wanted to be involved in.

Close-knit group of clients

The impact this work has is not easy to describe. We sponsor retirement parties where the client's friends all get to celebrate their friend's newly found freedom and yearn for the time that they will be enjoying the same feeling. You are the focal point, the person they will look to for help as they anticipate entering this most exciting part of their lives. This isn't a random collection of clients that make up your practice. On the contrary, it is a close-knit group of individuals, and your team is the fabric that holds it altogether.

Our annual Christmas party takes on almost a ballgame-type of atmosphere with retirees from several companies represented, all of them swapping stories about what they have in common and enjoying the fact that they won't be going to work in the morn-ing. You have become somewhat of a hero – and are being paid very well to fill that role. They bring their friends to the party so they can see what it will be like when they, too, no longer have to awaken and confront the rigors of the workplace.

You are now finding that you are involved in long-term care, estate planning, and Medicare supplements. You helped them walk away, and now your job entails protecting what they built, so the work just keeps coming to you. It isn't necessary to seek new clients, but because of the referral system you have continued to gain them nonetheless.

It's almost like a family, and you just have to nurture them; as you do the family continues to thrive. The long workweek you dreaded is long gone, and you find that even 40 hours isn't required anymore. But the financial rewards just keep on growing. The financial professionals who doubted that the concept would work now want to join your team. You are dealing with the fastest-growing segment of the population, those that are over 60, and it just keeps on getting better.

You were in the right place at just the right time. This wasn't serendipity or good luck! You acted on a simple truth: *If you want to stand out, you have to do something different.* AND YOU DID! (You notice I didn't say you did something extremely difficult. I just said it was different.)

Best of both worlds: Experience and youth

You are now beginning to add younger players to your team so they can take care of the client base that you built when you decide it's time join the ranks of those you have been serving with your own retirement. This becomes an unbeatable combination – your experience and their youth. Those you serve notice that once again you are ahead of the curve. It just keeps getting easier because you are riding the wave instead of fighting it.

You are now beginning to help your clients transition some of their wealth to charities. With the business of retiring them well in hand, you now get to play a small part in making the world a better place to live. With their money, no less!

The whole process is just a big circle and it all started when you recognized a hole that most in your profession didn't care to fill. There is no escaping it: It unquestionably seems at this point that *it just doesn't get any better than this.* And you're right – it doesn't.

Chapter Eleven:

THIS KIND OF BUSINESS WILL
CHANGE YOUR LIFE

Leaving a legacy that's priceless

There is no intent in this chapter to move from the business world into the arena of pure emotion. But the way we are wired makes it necessary for us to want to share our exciting experiences, and if we can't they just aren't that exciting.

The very beginning of this book indicates you can be very successful if you will simply channel your efforts into helping an individual leave the workplace. And the whole point of this book is to pass on what I have learned.

The very essence of our lives is based on this principle. We teach our children to follow ethical guidelines, hoping they will learn the lesson well and teach it to our grandchildren. The purpose of this book is to *CHANGE YOUR LIFE,* not because of the words written in it, but because of the concepts that changed mine. I have no doubt you will be successful in this business if you implement them.

But the greatest value of all for this book goes beyond introducing you to a concept that will change your life. There is also the desire to equip you with the ability to change *many* lives and therefore, to **LEAVE A LEGACY.**

The last chapter indicated, once again, that *it just doesn't get any better than this.* That phrase was talking about a mature business and the effortless success that has been experienced through implementing a unique concept. There is, however, one way that it does get even better – and that is when you become involved in the business of changing lives and creating legacies.

There is definitely something better about the opportunity to pass on principles and concepts that can change multiple lives, even multitudes of lives. That's what we want to discuss in this final chapter.

When the concepts we've been talking about work for you as they have for me, then you have an opportunity to experience something that transcends being financially successful: You have the opportunity to pass the knowledge down and *leave a legacy*. That's exactly what a parent does. The imparting of knowledge to their children ultimately is much more fulfilling than handing them a dollar.

Building your legacy, helping build others

So my goal has been to share what I have learned, and if you perform the functions listed in this book, you will have lots of opportunities to share them as well. You can help the widow whose husband took your advice and bought life insurance to provide for her. Then she has the opportunity to use some of the excess to purchase insurance on her life and ultimately, to bless the lives of her children and grandchildren.

As you are building your own legacy, you can become involved in helping others build their own legacies. The only thing that you need to remember is what I've have emphasized repeatedly: *Go with what brought you.*

When you find yourself building a legacy and enabling others in their own legacy-building process, it will be because you didn't follow the path most traveled. If you had, you wouldn't have been working with her husband at all, unless he had been an ultra-successful businessman. It's not necessary for you to reinvest all the funds she received, but you do need to help her to pass it on.

Believe me, the opportunity to create a legacy is so much more exciting than creating a short-term gain. But to do it, you have to take the "I" out of TEAM, which means you are no longer looking for today's headlines. Instead, you are looking for what makes tomorrow better because you were involved.

That doesn't always mean investing rollover money or, for that matter, doing anything that will benefit you in the short-term. It may mean explaining to the widow that she can pick up her husband's Social Security even though she is only 60, because she is entitled to a widow's pension. In doing so, you have just changed a life. You were in the right place at just the right time, and that is the kind of thing that ultimately creates a legacy.

You have the opportunity to show another younger person how they can find the secret – so that they in turn will continue to help the people that no one else wants to work with. We need to give without expecting to get anything in return; along the way you will discover that the joy of seeing others carry on this process has its own rewards.

Helping an eager group to give back

You are now helping a completely different group of people to give back to society. The standard approach – the "conventional wisdom" – has always been that the "Ultra-Rich" are the ones that leave trusts behind to help non-profits because they have funds in excess of what they can pass down to their children. You, on the other hand, chose not to build your practice around them. You have created a successful practice serving a very different area of society.

Why wouldn't planned endowments be something that would work in this area, just like everything else? The answer to that question is simple: It will. These individuals might not have monies enough to create death taxes, but you have worked with them long enough to know that they have funds *in excess of what they will spend in retirement.* You know this better than anyone because you helped them to plan their retirement; since then you have been helping them to manage it. Why would you not work with them at this point to give something back to someone other than their children at their death?

This is a game-changer, because just as no one except you realized their potential for helping to build and grow a financial planning practice, the same is also true about their capacity for leaving endowments. You created a practice built on a foundation that most of your peers didn't even realize existed. Why should you not now help society to receive a benefit from an area of endowments that they in turn didn't even realize exists?

The answer to this question is obvious. You can and will help make this happen, and that creates the legacy that's unmatched. There is no fund-raiser looking for this kind of person. They are the best-kept secret in the nonprofit world. You know the secret, you understand their potential – and you and you alone can help them reach their potential to make this world a better place.

Huge potential for change

We are only beginning to explore the *legacy* that can be left behind. You are working in an area that others have failed to recognize, and just like any other areas that were overlooked through the years, this creates huge potential for change.

The future for the financial professional who works with the common man is so exciting because, as stated before, this potential has never been tapped. To most financial professionals, it's invisible. The people that don't live in the upper echelons of affluence need you – while the "ultra-rich" do not. You can't change society by doing the same thing everyone else is doing, and most everyone else is working with the wealthy.

I will state once more: There is nothing wrong with that. Computers are still needed by big businesses, just as they always were, but Steve Jobs and Steve Wozniak turned the whole world on its ear by creating the personal computer. The concept was an alarmingly simple one; create a computer for the common man. What have we spent 11 chapters talking about? ***The concept is about doing financial planning for the common man.***

One has to ask oneself whether Apple was just trying to make society better. I think all of us would agree they did succeed at improving society, but we also know the rest of the story. They made a huge profit along the way. Helping to make a better world – and making money in the process. What's wrong with that?

When you do something unique, there are only two possible outcomes. The first is that when you are doing something different, you might fail. The second, of course, is that you might succeed. If this is the case, it will almost always be as it was with Apple – success on a much larger scale than you ever dreamed.

I think this brings us full circle. As we have said, the "secret" is there is no secret. You are simply working as a financial professional in an area that many would tell you is a waste of time. You must do something at this point that sometimes is very difficult: *DON'T LISTEN TO THEM.*

Nothing wrong with a head start!

You will find that eventually the financial industry will catch up, just as the technology industry did with the personal computer. This will take quite some time, however, and you already will have helped many people that others thought weren't worth the time. Your life will be changed because you changed the lives of so many.

I think you have probably noticed by now that this author doesn't think you can fail. I don't just *think* you will succeed – I think you will succeed ***beyond your wildest expectations.*** You are going to be a trailblazer, and blazing trails are much more fun than just following someone else.

Some of you have read this entire book and are still looking for something more. We have said time and time again that the concept is very simple. There *isn't* anything more. Here is one more example, however, which I hope will help in making the point. Hang with me for a few moments and you'll see what I mean:

The example is from the Bible: Naaman was a wealthy Assyrian general. He seemed to have it all, but he was dying of leprosy. He had tried all the normal techniques to find a cure, all to no avail. He finally gave in to a servant girl's plea to see a prophet in the country of Israel – the same Israel that Assyria had conquered years before. Naaman loaded up his donkeys with gold to give to the prophet, Elijah, and departed with his soldiers to find Elijah and perhaps buy his cure.

I am sure, although the Bible doesn't say this, that Naaman strongly felt this probably wouldn't work. But he was in fact a dying man, and dying men are willing to try desperate measures. He arrived at an area close to Elijah's home, after consulting the king of Israel for the prophet's exact location. Through the king, the military leader summoned Elijah to come out and meet with him.

Elijah, however, didn't go to meet Naaman. Instead, he sent his servant to tell Naaman to dip seven times in the Jordan River. The terminally ill Assyrian was told he would be cured forever of the dreaded disease if he simply followed these simple instructions. Dip seven times – no more, no less.

Naaman, however, was taken aback with what he was asked to do. He felt humiliated. He had never pictured it in this way, and that's not conjecture. The Bible plainly states that Naaman imagined he would give the prophet all his gold and that in turn Elijah would conduct an elaborate ceremony. He would wave his hands over Naaman during this ceremony and this would heal him.

When this scenario failed to play out as expected, Naaman was so prideful and hurt that he almost went back home, where he certainly would have died. However, once again, at the insistence of one of his servants, he swallowed his pride and, probably with some embarrassment, dipped himself seven times in a dirty river. The result: He was miraculously, fully cured.

The moral of this story: *Don't allow yourself to go back to "Assyria" with leprosy.* Do as you're told.

I tell you one more time, with the greatest assurance: These concepts might sound crazy, but **they do work!** Maybe you were looking for something more grandiose, more complicated, but this is it. And it's enough, I promise.

In closing, I wish you God's blessing and good luck. This is almost a misstatement, because you already have the blessing. It was there when you were born.

And as I said at the beginning, luck is something you simply won't need!

www.ingramcontent.com/pod-product-compliance
Lightning Source LLC
Chambersburg PA
CBHW051322170526
45166CB00002B/651